I0757397

The Liberation of Sue Moody
Slaying the Dragons

By

Gail Gelburd

Copyright ©2025, **Gail Gelburd, Massachusetts**

All rights reserved. No part of this publication may be reproduced. Distributed, or transmitted in any form or by any means, including photocopying, recording, or other electronic or mechanical methods, without the prior written permission of the author, except in the case of brief quotations embodied in critical reviews and certain other non-commercial uses permitted by copyright law.

First published by Hambone Publishing, 2025

Edited by Hambone Publishers

Cover design by Hambone Publishers

For information about this title contact through gailgelburd.com

Or email otishistoricalcommission@gmail.com

ISBN (paperback) 978-1-967864-11-9

ISBN (hard cover) 978-1-967864-10-2

ISBN (eBook) 978-1-967864-09-6

Library of Congress 2025944211

Dedicated to

Jesse, Joel

and those who have had a chance to meet Sue Moody

Contents

Preface & Acknowledgment

Sue Moody believed in fairy tales. She believed that a knight in shining armor, on a pristine white horse with a jeweled harness and bells, would come and scoop her up, and they would live happily ever after. He would slay all the dragons that terrified and belittled her and would make her feel like a princess. He would shower her with necklaces and gems and take care of her forever. The problem was how to reconcile the fairy tale with a desire to be a journalist and writer. Was there ever a knight in shining armor on a pristine white horse? She didn't know that there would be so many dragons in a woman's life and that she would have to slay them herself.

Sue Moody left behind, in a little house in rural Otis, Massachusetts, a treasure trove of journals, letters, manuscripts, and published articles. The crumbling boxes, in this long-since-abandoned house, are the story of her life. Some pages were fading, some were weathered, some were yellowing, and had aging brown spots. Some were legible, some were not. The letters from friends, colleagues, lovers, and family help to tell her story. Some of the people were famous, like Molly Brown; some were not. She wrote almost every day for decades as if someone would one day read this and know that she did exist! Each letter and poem once held a secret, a relationship, or a story. Each person had their own story. Each letter was anticipated when it arrived, ripped open, and devoured by the intended recipient. But she is not forgotten, for now you will know her story. This book is based on those materials.

Inside one large smashed-in cardboard box was another little box, still perfectly intact, with a broken necklace and the first poem she ever wrote. When we brushed away the dust and mold, it was beautiful. The necklace she made for herself was strung with a bead of brown, red, green, and blue glass beads. She saw them as topaz, ruby, jade, and turquoise. A simple, flowery rose hung in the center. She wrote a poem about this necklace in 1922 when she was at the beginning of her life and who she wanted to be. She had strung each bead onto the necklace, and each bead was so much more to her. How prophetic the little poem about her life. One hundred years later, this necklace was still in a precious box with her poem. Each precious gem represented a time in her life.

The Necklace
Long ago, she had hidden it far away.
She thought to play with it with love
but its fiery vibrant beauty
made her wonder
what had made her hide the necklace away

In all its glory, as she held it there

in the Moonlight against her fluffy black hair,

it trembled to breathe out a story.

Each gem in the necklace

was there by design

as a radiant link of life.

Slowly, with dark eyes wide open

she counted the beads

of her necklace.

A prayer for each,

a sigh for each jewel

that has lost its luster.

Turquoise:

like the baby blue violets

you'd have strewn in my path

and always sky's happiness

but a child's daisy chains

are forgotten.

Topaz:

True-eyed Gallant,

ever worthy to be of you

The Liberation of Sue Moody

ladies' hearts esteem.

came you to my feet

and nailed their kiss

to my hem

and made me feel

that the gift you had to offer

and it's Gladdening golden

was a jewel to wear forever,

Topaz makes me catch my breath

Then, half sobbing, I can smile

and hold her tight against my heart

and close my eyes

my days gleaned ever amber color

in mindful of that Topaz gem.

Emerald Green

Emerald, as I look at your passionate brilliance

even now I know why your sparkle bewitched me.

It lasts – –

when the world was green spring.

And you threw your Jewel

recklessly at my feet.

And took it back again

You gave the green emerald

and opals and diamonds and said

I was worth far more than that.

Ruby

a sweet tune I knew

and forgot

strains through my head

even now blended

with laughter and song

and a tear of love

but fear a ruby so red

and a promise

and the passion had fled

gone far from us

a Sweet tune I knew

and forgot

skims through my head

even now

But you lost our jewels

and I think you will no longer say

she's worth more than that.

The Pendant

A trembling circuit of frosted fire

why are you the secret of life

and are you a pendant of surety.

And as she sat on a sandbar by the lake

beneath a slowly purpling sky

to suddenly find her dreams

swished up and tossed on high,

like the pendant tossed in a drawer

and left to fade.

Similarly we sometimes only look at a house when it is pristine and dismiss the crumbling remnants of its life. We only see the glistening gems of a necklace and ignore how it was put together or why. We are blinded by what is supposed to be beautiful and perfect, failing to see how it all came to be. It goes full circle, and like life, we often come back to where we began, at the clasp that loosely holds it together. Along the length of the necklace, as in life, some moments stand out and define us. It might be a ruby or glass bead, topaz or jade that relates to different times. Or it might just be discarded glass. Is there a difference?

But I will let her tell her own story, mostly in her own words, and will merely fill in where needed, or to provide context for the events that ensued and colored her life. The necklace with beads of ruby, jade, turquoise, and a pendant will represent a different stage of her life. The necklace will form the structure of her story until it falls apart – and we must decide how to put the pieces back together.

I need to profoundly thank Marlyn Coffey for saving these items after Moody's house was left abandoned.

The Otis Historical Commission was then given these papers and, together with the Otis Preservation Trust, was instrumental in organizing, archiving the materials, and encouraging me to transform Sue Moody's story into a book. When I joined the commission, they were just at the early stages of this monumental task. I then read each page as they collated the materials. I need to especially thank Celeste Watman, Lynne Geane, Stephanie Skinner, Judi Mabee, Tricia Smith, Geoff Pigman for their tireless efforts. They read, commented, and edited my early drafts.

The town has also been supportive of this project, and I am proud to live in a town with such a rich history.

Sue Moody found this little town in Western Massachusetts to be one of incredible natural beauty and environmental activities. Amongst the trees, lakes, rivers, waterfalls, and ski slopes, it is also a haven for writers, artists, musicians, and those who care about culture but want to escape the big city. Midway between New York City and Boston, Otis has similarly proven to me to be the perfect retreat. I am proud to be able to offer this publication to those in Otis, but also to those who seek a place to breathe fresh air, paint, write, meditate, or grow fresh vegetables. After surviving the difficulties of being a female journalist in the US and then Hitler in France, Otis welcomed Sue Moody with open arms. Otis continues to do that.

Chapter 1
Ruby

Before the nightmare began, bright sunshine streamed down on us as we crossed the gangplank onto the ship. This was the vessel, I thought, that would make all my dreams come true. The sojourn from Kansas to NYC to Paris would enable me, a woman, to be a journalist. I was to be a food and fashion writer for United Press International in the most beautiful city in the world.

What a glorious time I thought we would have. My son, Bobby, was in tow, and he had to have our Springer Spaniel Mitzi with us. I wanted to share all of my Paris with him. I would take my son to museums and sidewalk cafes and be invited to dinner parties. I made a list of the best sites in Paris that I had been to before and was prepared to show my son the Bois de Boulogne, the grand boulevards, the Louvre, the gardens, and the Palace at Versailles. As we traversed the Atlantic Ocean, I told him stories of my Paris. I told him how nothing compares to the Palace of Versailles and its gardens. The bedroom of Louis Quinze had beautiful medallions of his four daughters. The room next to it had paintings by Boucher, who created sumptuous, alluring women. The exuberance of the Palace contrasted with the well-planned grounds that were laid out so perfectly that they seemed to be painted rather than planted. They reached out in every direction, like the spokes of a wheel. Stretching out as if they were avenues under the trees, they were trimmed like Gothic cathedral windows. I explained that we would spend most of an afternoon wandering down a path or cutting through the large trees, sitting in the shade. But for me, the prettiest place of all seemed to be where everything grew naturally, where a hamlet is located. The hamlet was the retreat of Marie Antoinette's ladies. When they were tired of the pressures of court, they would dress as peasants and go to live in a quaint little thatched cottage. It reminded me of a Corot painting. I wanted to one day be in that Corot painting, living in a little cottage by a lake. But first, I would write exciting food articles and become known for my unique articles. In Paris, I could readily add art and poetry to a food article, writing stories that became a part of people's lives. My enthusiasm and excitement were overwhelming, until the next day when we arose to find low dark clouds looming above, and waves fiercely lapping against the bow. Perhaps, I should have thought to turn around, but I had a job as a journalist in Paris! How bad could it be? What could go wrong?

The warnings began. I became constantly nauseous and dizzy. I could barely go out of my cabin. Meanwhile, Bobby so enjoyed the open sea and the ship. Everything would be fine. I labored in our cabin, as Bobby and Mitzi strolled the decks. Mitzie quickly became the star of the ship. She strutted down the promenade deck, her fluffy white and brown tail wagging as she was routinely pet by absolutely everyone on board. She walked slowly by the dining room, and people brought her scraps. If the band started to play music, she sat and attentively listened. Even the Captain would stop to pet her as she wagged her tail with vim and vigor. At night, she had to go back to the kennel where there was one other resident, a cat that howled incessantly the whole trip. She hated those loud noises and that cat, but how Mitzi loved the daytime of our trip. She would always hate loud noises. I miss her.

After eleven days, we descended the ramp of the boat in France. We strolled leisurely and excitedly off the ship. I decided that it would be nice to take a little walk in the garden of a nearby chateau. I had been seasick for so many days of the journey, but now I was on land, and not just any land. I was in France. I was still feeling a bit nauseated from the seasickness and not paying much attention, until suddenly I looked around more carefully and realized that something was not right. There seemed to be a lot of commotion. We walked the street to the garden, but it soon became very clear that there was a pervasive tension in the air.

Cars and trucks hurried by in every direction, not the casual stroll I was used to in Paris.

The city was in a feverish, depressed, and agitated mood. It was October 1939, and France had just declared war on Germany! Was I so oblivious to the facts that England and France would declare war on Germany after Germany invaded Poland? I heard someone say, "It is rumored that the Germans are actually not far from Rouen." There was a crowd in the square in front of Jeanne D'Arc's statue. "But they can't be coming this way!" A man named Bill protested. "Oh yes," leered a large, ugly man in the crowd, they will surround Paris, you know." "It is a fever of madness," cried another. There was deafening loud shouting, and people were worrying about bridges being destroyed up and down the Seine, or Notre Dame Cathedral being bombed. There seemed to be a roar of smoke and military in the distance. The first man, Bill, now stood there quietly, afraid, a desolate wreck. He sat down on a bench and sobbed. We looked around in disbelief and hurried to get a taxi to our apartment that United Press International (UPI) rented for us. It was on the 5th floor in the Paris suburb of Meudon. I told Bobby that we will figure it all out once we are settled.

After all, I had my dream job. Writing about food and fashion in Paris, the center of it all. I decided that even war couldn't take this away from me. I waited so long for this opportunity. At the beginning of the War, I talked to French women every day at the post office as they sent out packages of food and knitted things for their menfolk who were far from home. I read what they said in every French newspaper and magazine. One article written by a newspaper columnist praised the women who were organizing the relief efforts and the nurses. The column that struck me the most was devoted to the encouragement of women who took the burden of making things run smoothly at home. These were the lesser-known feminists looking after the old people and children. They were the heroines who helped the town to maintain an even tenor instead of becoming panic-stricken.

My first columns for UPI declared to the women of France, "You are as brave as the finest Red Cross nurse in the whole land. You are working without honor or glory. If before you enjoyed feasts and evenings together, enjoy something today with your friends, even if it is only a cup of tea with milk in the afternoon, while the children are gathering for their cocoa."

I thought the families and soldiers needed a boost to their morale. Women complained about how the men were broken; they all needed their spirits lifted. United Press International agreed that I must do exactly that. I wrote hundreds of joyous articles about cooking, recipes, and entertainment. After all, that was what a woman was expected to write. I wrote that families should take out their little garden chairs and tables, even if it was cold outside. That did not last long. Who sits in the garden as bombs fall or Germans march outside your building? I was so naïve.

Instead, I had written in my article, "Everyone knows what it takes to bake a cake in hot weather. With war work relief efforts and the boys at camps, you won't have time for these 'informal' affairs of sandwiches and cake. Save your energy and save your money for patriotic causes. But we can still have get-togethers. Bake four kinds of cookies each day and put them in elegant boxes to send in the mail to the boys. Save some for your neighbors or those who do not have boys at the camp, or for a meeting of committee work, and enjoy a cheerful little gathering. Laying out a box of 4 cookies may not seem like enough at first, but if your spirit goes hand in hand with your joy of baking, it will work wonders for everyone. Every woman and man who stops by your house will be inspired to do their little projects. It will matter little if they only get 4 or even 2 cookies with a good, tall drink. Make a festive drink with lemons and fruit juices that you have on hand. A little tea added will not destroy its flavor, while it cuts the price in two.

For example, in a big jug put:
4 cups grape juice

4 cups medium-strength iced tea

2 cups honey syrup, honey melted in a little water

¾ lemon and some lemon peel

If you want to put out little sandwiches, there are two that are inexpensive, quick, and easy. One is made from cold cuts or good baloney with a sweet green tomato pickle. Just a combination of the two in exactly the right proportion put between buttered slices of white bread. The other is of a sandwich, cheese spread, and several leaves of lettuce. They are both so simple, and oh so good. Send out a little invitation to different people each day. Make the envelope by simply folding some khaki-colored paper three ways. Finish the envelope with a seal, be it Red Cross, or a red circular motif, Star seal, anything that is good with the pale cream-colored khaki paper. Slip the paper invitation inside. Each should be carefully written in your finest penmanship."

That was my job. Transform the blue light into a golden yellow glow of joy. Yellow and blue make green, and that was better than the dark blue mood that engulfed the city and the people.

Every day back then, I also made some biscuits and chocolate for Bobby and three of his friends. Until there was no more chocolate, no more afternoons of hot steaming cocoa and tea. The sorrows now filled the air as families failed to hear about their husbands, fathers, sons, and brothers. But those days of afternoon repasts seemed unforgettable when we were later huddled, starving, and sick together. We often laughed about the days that we had squandered all that chocolate. We longed for those days. Suddenly, we heard shouting in the street, and someone yelled out that the cannons had been moved from the Place des Invalides. The Germans were coming.

Life changed dramatically. Those next months were anything but a sojourn of museums and parties, rather, it was filled with fear and anticipation of the unknown. Young men, fathers, brothers, sons were gone, off to fight. I lay in bed listening to the bombs falling around us and big guns going full blast back at them. It was all happening just a few miles away, on the outskirts of Versailles, and the two towns next to us. Our large apartment building shook, and Mitzi came up to me shivering in the dark. The whites of her big brown eyes stared out. She jumped onto the bed and slithered between my feet. Next, Bobby came running in, "Mommy, mommy, I am afraid, what is that noise? I am so afraid." "Bobby, we don't have to go outside, those are not sirens for us to go to the shelters. We are staying in our beds right now with the blackout curtains pulled tight." He was soon fast asleep, my soothing words comforted him. He believed that I knew how to protect him. I wish that I believed it. I stayed up all night long with Mitzi at my feet and Bobby curled up and snuggled next to me.

Yes, I was in Paris, a mother without a husband during a war. The eerie silence on the side streets was striking. Every child who could be sent to the countryside had gone. Some were in private homes, some with their grandparents. Mothers and older women often left with the children to do whatever they could; city women around Burgundy helped with the grape harvest. More than half the population of Paris had left, and the town had a dark and dreary feeling now. Many houses were completely shuttered already, shopkeepers covered their windows with crisscrossed strips of gummed reinforcement paper to prevent them from being broken and prevent anyone from looking into the windows. Add to this the blue paint covering many of the windows and doors so that at night, a light could be used inside and would not shine outward in case of bombings. Streetlamps were also covered with a dense blue paint, and there was scarcely any light if you strolled the streets at night. A profound silence soaked into the very fabric of your being. It was always dark except for this eerie blue glow. The blue glow permeated your whole being as you tried to keep the fear from spilling. There was nothing to do, no one to speak to now, and the profound silence seeped into your bones.

How funny to think that one day back in late November, at about 4 or 5 o'clock, I decided I needed to buy a new hat. The things that you worry about when you refuse to face what is happening. I wanted some semblance of normalcy. I went weaving my way through the greenish-blue streets of dimly lit images. I couldn't locate any of the shops that I knew. I couldn't look in the shop windows to see what they might have. It was difficult to find my footing even on major boulevards like St. Germain. The painted lamps gave the world a ghostly appearance as they began to come on. I let out a brief scream as a man on a bicycle rode by wearing a red jacket. He stood out for a moment and was then gone. I really wanted a hat, a sense of the Paris I knew from the 1920s. After all, Paris was not known as a commercial business area or war machine. Why invade France? It was the power and beauty that built Chartres, Notre Dame, Versailles, and the gardens. It was the Louvre Museum and the artists painting along the Seine. Paris was a city of fashion, wine, paté, fine breads, and cheeses. I bought a beautiful hat near the Palace of Versailles when my Paris was still Paris, a decade ago, but now there were no longer any shops. Being in Paris with a new hat would make me feel elegant. I wanted that again, but now I could not even find any kind of hat at all. A hat! I worried about a hat, and now I would give up all my hats to stop the noise.

All we could hear were whistling, whirling sounds, crashing explosions, sirens screeching warning us—but where do we run to? Then silence was interrupted by children screaming, women's muffled weeping; the gripping fear of another bombardment in your belly was never far away. No place to go, no way to escape from these sounds, except to hopelessly cover your ears. It was worse than a hundred cats screeching in the night. Every minute was the anticipation of the sound of another plummeting bomb and then the reverberating explosion. An aviator tossed five or six bombs out of his plane right near our building, demolishing, flattening homes, and killing men, women, and children indiscriminately. Lives that were meant to be lived. Young men, women, and children, lives that struggled with intimate and happy moments at another time, while working in offices or on farms. They brought home presents and treats when they could afford it, or flowers for their mother as they saved up for a new used car or a little vacation. These were lives not yet fully lived. These were the people who, in the flash of a moment, were killed by the bombs. I knew that I had to survive; I had to live my life somehow. I had to save my child, save myself.

After days of continuous bombings, it suddenly stopped. It was June 14, 1940, and now Mitzie was barking incessantly, and 8-year-old Bobby ran into my room. I tried to quiet them both, their barking, chattering, I couldn't hear what was going on. "People will hear you," I yelled, "Stop." Then I remembered that the huge building, that we were in, was empty, deserted, and no one would hear any of us. Five families of the 22 that lived in our building originally were all that remained. And even they were now packing up their lightest suitcases as they tried to leave Paris. They were lucky if they had their car. There were no taxis, trains, or cars available in Paris. The Germans were approaching, would they let them leave? Should we have left? Could we? We were Americans, and America was helping the French and British. We couldn't risk getting caught.

It was 6 am when Bobby began shouting, and Mitzie barking. Their sounds echoed into the darkened halls, kitchens, and abandoned bedrooms where only the remnants of people's lives remained. Clothes were left strewn in the empty apartments, kitchen cabinets had been left open and emptied, and broken China lay on the floors. Mitzie ran to the windows, so I finally drew the courage to look out our apartment window. Our building was now surrounded by German troops. I grabbed my press pass and put the cord around my neck in case they came in. I was a journalist; they wouldn't harm me and my family, right? I thought that my Press pass would be my warrior's shield. I clutched it tightly in my hand. I quieted Mitzie and told Bobby to stay away from the window. I didn't know what to do next. I was shaking with fear. What do you do when the bombs are falling, and the German troops are parading past your window? When you have a child, displays of fear and a showering of tears are just not an option. I had to do something. So, I did what every mother and housewife in the 1930s was expected to do: I began to scrub the floor, the cabinets, and clean every inch of the apartment. I sang happy tunes as I cleaned to drown out the sound of the marching troops below, the sound of rolling vehicles, horses, and the pounding of footsteps in unison. My singing got louder, although sometimes it was broken, as I held back tears. For hours, it went on, and on, and on; rolling troops, cleaning, singing, scrubbing as if I could wash it all away.

A horrible fear crept up over me, and the eerie silence in the apartment and the whole building resonated inside of me. The only sound was the rolling of the trucks and guttural German commands. As I stood in the kitchen, I thought about whether we should have left or now leave, or could we even go outside if we needed something? What would happen if they found us? I looked at the few cans left in the cupboard: three stacks of cans, ten or twelve evaporated milks, peaches, pears, and a few green peas, a couple of cans of pork and beans. For breakfast, we ate a plain piece of bread, sometimes with a cup of hot water with a beef bouillon cube that I rustled up a few weeks before. One cube would go for 4 cups of hot water. Once in a great while, I found a shredded wheat biscuit for Bobby to eat with plain hot water and a little bit of powdered milk sprinkled on top. I had, by great fortune, found 2 packages of shredded wheat in an English grocery store that opened its doors for two days to sell out its contents. Maybe we had enough for two weeks, three if we stretch it out. What would we do then? The stores were all closed. It took me more than a month to accumulate this amount. There was a limit to what I could carry home and then up those five flights of stairs since the elevator was no longer running, and I was so weak. How long would we last? All the houses and buildings up and down the street were shuttered. Everyone seemed to have left. I had two sugar cookies remaining in a jar. They were yellow stars with pointed edges and a sprinkling of nuts and cinnamon just over the center. I think that they are called Nuremberg cookies. How ironic to only have a German named cookie left.

I came to Paris because of what I thought was the opportunity of a lifetime. I was hired by the United Press International (UPI) to write about French food and fashion. Now, my life was reduced to a few cans and a German cookie. How ironic that my job was to write about food when there was none. Could I put together an interesting recipe of bouillon, evaporated milk, pork and beans, and peaches?

Distressed from looking at our remaining cans, I ran to the other window, on the other side of the apartment. From these windows, I could see Paris spread out before me in the dappled early morning sun. The city, thought by many to be the most beautiful in the world, stood, from my vantage point, to be exactly as it had been before the Germans came. The boulevards radiated out from the center, past the gardens, emulating Versailles. They were laid out like a flock of white and grey birds in long lines over the hills. *Sacre Coeur* stood as serene as ever, a toadstool on a distant hill. White Grecian pillars of two other buildings stood like temples in the sunlight along the way. The river still wound like a silver ribbon down the valley.

I wanted to show my son my Paris and brought him with me when I got this job, so I could show him my Paris. But now I couldn't show him anything but fear. Perhaps, my Paris was gone forever. I sat in the kitchen remembering how Johnny and I strolled a decade earlier along the streets, looking inside courtyards, and through open doorways where I could glimpse Parisian living. We saw magnificent statues, beautiful white nude lovers entwined in one another's arms, ignoring all those who walked by, while off to the side, a couple of young lovers embraced. The statues never seemed to get cold, even when the flowers were gone, and when the snow fell on them, matching their whiteness, they still exuded warmth. It is said that the heat of their passion and the comfort of their embrace protect them from all icy blasts. Were there still such lucky statues that they can catch and hold the most beautiful things in life, and never change? I wondered if there was a way to be frozen in time, back in a moment of joy and love. Could I return to that moment?

Johnny and I wandered carefree through the streets when we were there in the 1920s, sampling each cafe, restaurant, and Bistro. All the meals were simply extraordinary, with subtle, explosive tastes at each bite. Each morsel was enticing. A lunch would consist of *hors d'oeuvres*, mostly cold meats, fish, ham, calves' brains, and morsels of veal. Then, the waitress would announce that she would bring the meat course, which consisted of chicken, salad, cheese, and bread. And then a huge bowl of chocolate mousse for us to share. My stomach grumbled from hunger as I reminisced about the Parisian cafes. Now we barely had a piece of bread. I thought my Paris must survive. Would I ever get to share it with Bobby? He woke me from my daydream, shouting that he wanted to go outside and see my Paris.

Perhaps I had calmed Bobby's fears too much, as now he didn't seem to quite understand the dangers. He suddenly saw it as a great big parade. He didn't want to stay still or be quiet any longer and declared that his friend's mother was across the street and that she was sick. "I must go find Renee." "Are you mad?" I replied. "Don't you understand that those are Hitler's men down there? You are staying right here in our kitchen." The kitchen had always been our special safe space, and now he was running from it. He pulled his pants on over his pajamas and yelled, "But I can't. Renee has no food; his Mama might be dying. Don't you care?" I replied, exasperated, "What! Wait, please, no, don't go, no, you must stay here." Bobby had been coming into the house with all kinds of stories for the last couple of weeks, but I guess that I hadn't listened very well. He had told me that everyone was leaving town or getting ready to leave, to go to the country, to farms anywhere, away from here, to a place with food. He said to me, "They won't stay and wait for the Germans to come and kill them." He kept telling me that we should leave. He was right. I knew. But what could we do? We had both seen the procession of people leaving our Parisian suburb every day. "Please, Mommy. Renee's father is a soldier, and they haven't heard from him in over three weeks. She doesn't have any money; they don't even have any jam left." Jam, I didn't know what any of this had to do with jam. "And his mom has been sick in bed for a week." I held onto his capuchin, that long cape with a hood that the schoolboys in France wore to protect them from the rain. He pulled towards the door. I again tried to be rational and explain that the Germans hate English people. They hate Americans even more because we are helping the English and the French. "You will get caught and start speaking English. You will land us both in prison or worse. I simply cannot let you go. You must not go out." I grabbed him, but he broke away. He was so strong and disobedient. He ran into the hallway. And defiantly said. 'No, Mom. I will speak French, not English. I won't talk to them at all. Just to Renee. You taught me French since I was very little. I will speak only French." "Bobby, Bobby, come back." I yelled, "No, please no." Bobby was gone, with Mitzie running after him. "I yelled after him, "Please, stop, I won't let them starve, but please not now…" He was off down the stairs, and they were gone. I ran to the window to see if I could spot them leaving the building. There was a sea of Khaki and Gray, covered wagons and men unhitching their horses. The men were tying them to the iron bars of a high grille that surrounded our garden.

Across the street and down the block was a large military hospital. Groups of German soldiers passed our windows every hour. There was a small wooden house on the corner next to us, empty. Soldiers seemed to be searching for something. Finally, they found two buckets and filled them with water at the faucets by our rose bushes. I held my breath. Just then, a troop of cavalry came by, shouting commands, and I could hear the sounds of a squealing horse a block away on the Boulevard Republique. Next came, Scouts with their steel helmets riding on motorcycles and yelling commands in German. I was five floors above the commotion, but where was Bobby? He was nowhere to be seen in the crowd of khaki-clad bodies. The scene before me was like a circus with hordes of people. When you lose someone in a crowd like that, you can never find them. What if he had climbed into one of those covered trucks? After all, he was just a mischievous young boy. No, don't think that, no, he is smarter than that. I left the window and fell back into bed, sick to my stomach. A few minutes later, I was back at the window. They kept filing past the building entrance, a sea of German uniforms. I searched desperately for Bobby's head, and Mitzie's white, fluffy tail. I could not find either. On and on the soldiers marched. It was never-ending. The rumble and roar of the trucks and vans, and motorcycles. It was a parade that, in another circumstance, I might have thought was intriguing to watch.

I went back to the kitchen, our safe space, and sat on the stool next to where Mitzie usually sat, looking for scraps. Mitzi always learned new tricks with pieces of bread or a stick for bait. Bobby and I always found the kitchen to be the coziest place in the whole house. Watercolor paints were still on the floor just before I cleaned everything away. It seemed like only yesterday that the tea kettle was singing and Renee was telling long stories in his bubbling fast fast-paced French. Now, the kitchen was the most dreaded room in the house. All around us, pots and pans hung from the ceiling rack; pots and pans that should have been filled with steaming hot food, except that there was no real food to be had.

I could not even think that the children and Mitzie had run off! How could they? Where were they? What should I do? I felt helpless. I paced; the minutes seemed like hours.

I went and looked out of each window to see if I could see them. One window had a great view of the City of Paris. It was a tremendous relief to find Paris not bombed, unspoiled, and so tranquil in her loneliness, as if she were unaware of the terror surrounding her. Of course, the suburbs and some factories, as well as many towns along the way, had been destroyed. But Paris itself was still there, the City of Beauty and Lights. I almost forgot for a moment the roar of the cannons on the other side of the apartment, or those instruments of destruction that were rolling past my window.

I sat huddled in a corner, trembling, singing, scrubbing occasionally, and listening to the Germans and for the sounds of

Mitzie and Bobby. The dismaying realization that there was not enough food for those already living in this occupied zone, and the German soldiers would take whatever was there. The terror of more bombardments continued as well. Surely, Bobby and Mitzie must be hiding somewhere safe. They must be. What I would give for just one of those cookies right now, but instead we will save them as the last vestiges of civilization.

Suddenly, there was a large commotion in the hallway, and I heard Mitzie barking. Bobby and Renee stood there motionless as I flung open the door. Two little fugitives with white, smudged faces, their "capuchins" splotched with mud. I hugged them both as tightly as I could, while Mitzie jumped up and down. Then I peeled them off of me and screamed, "Where have you been? How could you run off like that?" "Rue de la Republique," sputtered Renee in his fastest French. "We saw Hitler!" "What!" "We saw Hitler! "Je m'en fous de Hit-ler!" "Bobby," I screamed. "Hitler! Hitler! Hitler with his little painted moustache and twenty-five steel-armored cars and trucks with soldiers in them following right behind. There he was, Mom! There he sat. He just sat there and looked at us!" "Madame," Renee, bursting with excitement, said, "It was really Hitler!" I almost fainted and grabbed them again as close to me as I could. I helped take off their cape. I begged the two urchins to sit down and stay. I asked them to please never go out onto the sidewalks when the Germans were there. Mitzie curled up in a corner, obviously exhausted from the adventure. Poor little dog. She ran after them to every place they went that day.

I tried to keep them in the house so that they could now recover. I was afraid to let them out of my sight. But as young boys, they were fascinated by the military and were always looking for the Generals and Hitler on the street below. Then again, somehow, when my back was turned, they ran out and crossed the street to Renee's house, where I could see little Giselle, his baby sister, sitting in the sun by the window sill. From down below, I suddenly heard a scream. "Mom, Mom," screeching, shouting. I grabbed my coat and ran down the steps. Bobby quickly said, "It's Renee's mother; she is very sick." I had been sending over little cheese balls that I made when Renee would go home. Had he shared them or eaten them himself? Inside the apartment, Renee's mother was wiping tears from her eyes. She held up a jar of jam that I had given her weeks before. It was in an apple butter jar. There was a spoon in it, but no jam. She cried, "This is all we have eaten for days, with some scraps of stale bread." I didn't have enough food for all of us for very long either. I thought about breaking into the empty apartments. But what if the people came back thinking that they had some food there? I thought while scheming ways to feed us. Renee's mother kept brushing Gisele's hair, pinning curls on the top of her head with beautiful barrettes. Now, she began to brush her long hair with a beautiful brush that had a mother-of-pearl handle. We were mesmerized as she brushed it and then braided her long hair.

I was a journalist in Paris. Surely, there was something that I could do. But I was a mother alone in Paris in the middle of a war, with hardly any food. What are my priorities? There was nothing that I could do. Why did I ever come to Paris? I convinced myself that we would be fine. Azalea bushes were beginning to flower in the back of the building, and it made me think of Charlie Phelps' house on a lake in Otis, a cottage by the woods near a lake in a small town in Western Massachusetts. Whenever I get sad or anxious, I visualize Charlie's house. I longed for that moment of quiet, of a small, intimate place of my own. I imagined myself sitting by the little pond in the garden, quietly reflecting on times and places gone by. It was my little cottage in the woods, like in the Corot painting.

Chapter 2
Turquoise

Some days, when I was in Kansas or Jackson Hole Wyoming or Otis Massachusetts, I would try to find myself by going to a pond as the sun started to rise, sitting on the edge of the pier, watching the pink lights fade from people's homes on the mountains. Stars and trees were reflected in the water, and they all looked so perfect in their reflections, so calm. I could sit there for hours. I would just kick my feet in the water and watch my shoes fall in the mud. As the water moved and the sun rose, my reflection seemed to disappear. What was left was just ripples of the sky, the trees, and me. I sat until I was damp and cold. A chill came over me as the night air took over. I gathered up my "kicks" and returned to my cabin, wherever it might be. By the end of summer, the mountains of Massachusetts or Wyoming were so majestic, and the trees had a few touches of gold on the tips of their branches. It was as if a painter was beginning his canvas and had dabbed here and there, before putting on vast splashes of color. Nature was my refuge, be it in Kansas, the Bois de Boulogne, or a little garden in Paris with some azaleas blooming.

It gave me such joy to reflect upon those images of my favorite places in the world. Milan Kundera wrote, "You think that just because it's already happened, the past is finished and unchangeable? Oh no, the past is cloaked in multicolored taffeta, and every time we look at it, we see a different hue[1]." I thought of those words as I reminisced about my early days of freedom and power, where I came from, and where I have gone. But then I thought of how the images disappear when my feet graced the pond and sent ripples through the images, through my memories. My old journals and letters, stored away in boxes, recorded my earlier memories and painted with words my life's adventures. They are the memories.

The summer before my last year of college, I began my journey to find a place where I could belong, a place where I could find myself. I had a family member who was a part-owner in the Bar B C Ranch in Jackson Hole, Wyoming. I dreamed of how nice it would be to be on my own, to ride horses, and share stories with the other writers that frequented that very special ranch. I loved brushing the horses, and then they nuzzle you for more. I even looked forward to shoveling out their stalls. It would be like I accomplished something. I hoped there would be new people to meet, and most of all, some freedom, and independence. Mother waved goodbye as I boarded the train. She reminded me to always be a "lady". And with those last words, I started what would be

---

[1] Milan Kundera, Life is Everywhere, (Harper Perennial, 1976), p. 140

the beginning of my new life. Be a lady! What does that mean when you are riding horses, and slinging hay and mud? Should I be a lady as I am raking out the horse manure from the stall, fill a wheelbarrow, and take it to the big pile of stinking hot deteriorating remnants of life. And did I really care about what anyone thought? Not at that time, not for that brief moment in my life. Could I still be a lady when life is slinging the manure at you?

I guess that a part of me did still think about "being a lady" as I entered Victor, Idaho, and searched the street for my hotel. Right there in front of me was the Killpatrick hotel, which they had told me to stop at when I got off the bus. The paint was peeling, and everything was dirty. An even filthier, anemic-looking gal in a dressing gown and worn-out, sloppy slippers approached to give me my room key. I was so proud of myself that I was going to work for the summer at this very special ranch for riding and writing. I was used to mucking stalls and sleeping in hay when I worked after school at the Lawrence riding academy. But for the first time in my life, I was on my own, no one could tell me what to do, or how to dress. As I looked around at this place, this supposed hotel, I knew that I would rather be sleeping in a stall, intoxicated by the smell of sweating horses and manure, any place but this, any place where I didn't have to worry about "being a lady". The ranch manager informed me that the Kilpatrick was the only hotel in Victor, Idaho, and that I should stay overnight until the next day, when the mail stagecoach could take me over the mountain to the ranch. It seemed that in June, the road was still not passable to cars. I wondered how snowy the roads were still at this time of year. I decided to go to the telegraph agent, before I went to my room, to send my mother a telegraph that I had arrived safely. There sat a colicky baby screaming and fussing so much that I could not even talk to them about my telegram. The telegraph agent was no better, and I spent an hour waiting for them to send it for me and then get a reply. Finally, the BC ranch got back to me to say that I could take the mail stage over the mountain and that they would meet me in Wilson to take me to Jackson Hole because it was impassable by car. I guess I was stuck staying at that hotel.

Two hours later, I stumbled back to the crumbling, dilapidated building, ready to lie down after my long trip. As I walked in the door, I was confronted by an old, half-toothless travelling salesman. He had been sitting there for a long time, because I noticed him when I first walked into the building, sitting in the same spot. He yelled out to me and told me how he wanted to make my stay in Victor "enjoyable". I was terribly rude to him, but he seemed used to it. I was scared to death now because, in fact, he was the only friendly person in the entire place. What did they think of me, coming from the big city of Lawrence, Kansas, to this place of cowpunchers and poorly dressed, homely pregnant wives? I really was not nice to these people, and what did I know of their lives or problems? I acted superior to them, but would soon be put in my place. The salesman must have been lonely because he spoke to me endlessly as I tried to ignore him. His conversations were inappropriate and made me feel very uneasy. "Where is your husband?" "You look so pretty in that dress, it accentuates your breasts." "How long are you staying here?" I tried to ignore these comments and kept walking away, pretending I didn't hear a word that he said.

I really just wanted to lie down, but when I went upstairs, I discovered there was no lock on my door. So, I decided to sit in the lobby for a while longer, despite the endless bantering of the salesman. I realized that I could make the most of this day by grabbing a pen and paper and writing notes about all the people that I saw there. After all, if I was going to be a writer, which was my dream, then I should be writing. This place was full of material. The salesman, seeing me back in the lobby, immediately came over to chat. I tried to ignore him again, and thought that he couldn't be successful at all with the way he looked and badgered a woman he didn't know.

Just as I was about to go take a walk, someplace, anyplace, a big fat middle-aged cowpuncher walked in with a young lean brown eyed cowpuncher, and two youngsters about eight and ten. They were all covered with worn leather chaps and spurs on their aging boots. They each wore large Mexican sombreros and colorful blankets across their chest. They reminded me of the Mad Hatter in Alice in Wonderland, swallowed up in these big hats. The thought of them as part of the Mad Hatter court made me chuckle aloud. As I snorted a little when I laughed, the two children, whose names I later learned were Jiggs and Wes, turned towards me before they ran to their older brother, whom they called Thau. The large older man was referred to as Dad by all three. Thau seemed to walk around the lobby, assessing the situation. He saw my bored face and the obnoxious salesman bothering me. Thau, who I thought was just a little older than me, saw the man bothering me and soon came over, sat down, and started talking to me. He interrupted the salesman every time he spoke, especially when he said something inappropriate. Finally, when the salesman wouldn't stop talking, he asked me if I wanted to go to the corner drugstore for an ice cream. I was so happy to get out of there, I forgot about being nervous, about going off with someone whom I had just met. He seemed nice enough, and hopefully, we were really going to an ice cream parlor. The drugstore had a grey worn counter with round red stools. I took a stool where the red linoleum wasn't peeling too badly. There was yellow foam sticking out from the torn linoleum stool cover. They only had two flavors of ice cream, but they had nuts and sprinkles, and syrup. As we sat eating from a big glass parfait cup, a large scoop of chocolate ice cream with nuts on top, Thau asked me if I wanted him to send that traveling salesman out of town. I said, "Sure," never thinking that he would. But within two hours, the obnoxious, rude man was gone. What did he say to him? Did he threaten him? Thau did have a big gun on his side. Perhaps I really was now in the Wild West, and I should be wary of men carrying big guns and what I ask them to do! Sometimes they could certainly be useful. I certainly could have used Thau as the Germans marched into Paris. But could he even save me?

Thau would become my knight in, well, sombrero armor that summer, accompanied by his two squires, Jiggs and Wes. It turned out that the three of them were going over the mountain where they would drive thirty head of cattle to Jackson Hole. I told them why I was going there and how I would have to wait overnight for the mail coach. It turned out that their dad had to head back to Blackfoot so that I could take his horse and saddle and ride with them over the mountain. My trunk was still by the telegraph agent, and at first, the telegraph agent wouldn't let me open it up to get my riding clothes. I begged him while the poor baby screamed and hollered. Finally, I suggested that he put a little whiskey on the colicky baby's gums, as I had seen my aunt do back home. The whisky bottle quickly appeared, and the baby was gulping the alcohol. After a few minutes, the baby quieted, and I asked again if I could get my riding gear. He was so thankful that he let me get out my gear and promised to send the trunk with the mail coach the next day.

We were off. At first, we rode slowly, and I felt free and safe with Thau and Wes, and Jiggs. We made it to Wilson that first day, but no one was there to meet us, and although we asked around, no one from the ranch was to be found. I thought that now I was really stranded and there were no hotels in the little town of Wilson. Fortunately, Thau knew the ranch that I was going to and agreed to take me to Jackson Hole. It was a 36-mile ride in total. It was glorious and beautiful, but exhausting. You can only imagine how I tumbled into a bedroll on the ground, somewhere between Idaho and Wyoming, by 8:30 at night. I wasn't used to riding so much, I wasn't used to the saddle, or the horse bucking every once in a while, either. Every muscle and bone in my arms, thighs, and rear ached. Riding through the mountains of Idaho and Wyoming through snow and over rocks was breathtakingly beautiful, but difficult. It was very different from the plains of Kansas, where I grew up and rode. The only mountain in Lawrence was the Odeon

Hill, where the University stood. Hardly a mountain compared to what I now saw. I wondered how I would survive the summer if I had to ride that much. Every inch of my body ached from just one day!

I slept so solidly on the ground that at 7:00 the next morning, the boys had to throw things at me to wake me up. They already had a fire going with coffee ready in an old, rusted, sooty black pot. We had a few muffins from the hotel, which they had in a bag. Within half an hour, we were back on the horses. The next set of trails to the ranch were even more narrow and treacherous. As we rode through the woods, making our path, it was hard not to feel like I was in another world. It was wild, untamed country, but absolutely magnificent. The trees brushed against my legs, and I ducked under branches. We walked, trotted, then ran the horses, and then got off and walked them again when the trail narrowed. I knew that I would have to paint the landscape with words and find a way to describe what I had seen. But it would have to wait until I wasn't so exhausted. We took a few detours and arrived at another ranch to stop to trade, and get some food. I must say that each person I saw at these ranches looked like they had fox or bear faces. Each one looked like a different animal, maybe from living in the woods so long. They, like the animals, survived the long, cold winters, focusing on food and warmth. I wondered what animal face I might have by the end of the summer. I remember wondering if I could survive without steady meals and a warm bed. What would I do if I had to forage for my meals? I stopped myself from thinking like this because surely a ranch where people pay good money to stay would have food and nice beds. This would not be the time that I had to scour the countryside for food. That would wait a decade for Paris.

I traveled through the woods and snow with my knight and his two squires. Whenever we would stop, he would leave us to tie up the horses. Thau would tell the kids to look out after me. He would then go on about how Jiggs and Wes were responsible for my safety while he was gone, even if it was just for an hour or so. When he returned, Thau told us all to start riding ahead and that he would catch up. Jiggs was just the sweetest boy I've ever met. If I ever had children (which back then I had no plans of ever doing), I hoped that they would be as sweet as him. Jiggs and I were jogging along nicely, and I was enjoying the scenery and the slower pace than the day before, when suddenly, I heard a whoop and clatter of hoofs, and my horse just tore out from there. I tried to slow my horse down, but he was following the others. I had to suddenly shift my seat and tuck my thighs hard to grip the horse. I tried to bear down on my heels as I pulled back on the reins, but it was no use. I then realized that there was a horse behind me going even faster, which made my horse buck a little and fight my reins. In an instant, I found myself ripped from my saddle and seated on another horse. Thau came galloping by on his horse, which was much faster than mine, grabbed me from my saddle, and in one fell swoop put me on his horse with him. I was terrified, shaking. I couldn't catch my breath for at least a mile, and when I did, I started screaming at him. I called him every name that I could think of, even though the young boys were within earshot. I would not act like a lady! I was just furious, terrified, and screaming. At first, Thau and the boys just laughed. "I thought that you would have liked going fast," said Thau. I kept screaming at him until he apologized, stopped his horse, put me down, grabbed my horse, and put me back onto it. We were perfectly silent for over an hour until we reached the ranch. Then, he came by and said contritely, "I guess you think that I'm quite a guy." "No, I don't, I yelled back, and I did not think that was funny." So much for a knight in a sombrero.

I should have realized then that no such thing exists. No knight in shining armor or a sombrero will ever rescue you. Little girls are told those lies so that they behave and act like a lady. After weeks of him showing up at the ranch, I gradually forgave him and we talked, and walked around the ranch, or sat on a bench for a while. He warned me about certain people at the ranch and then offered his services if I ever needed a gunman. He was heading back to Blackfoot to face his fate. He told me how he had never met a girl like me and that I scared him. I scared him? He told me his story of how he was befriending a native girl, but soon realized that they did not like outsiders in their community. They went to beat up Thau, but he got the better of them, and now the sheriff was looking for him. Thau had a reputation for beating up anyone who got in his way. I fear that he would kill the sheriff if the sheriff came for him, or he would get killed. Poor Thau. He was so sweet, for a bad man. It seemed that he might have killed someone in self-defense, and this other woman, who must be my age, was now suing him for divorce. Divorce. That meant that they were already married at my age. It was complicated, and I never did get the whole story. He had been hiding out in the hills when he met me. Killing, divorce, and I thought that he was no older than I. I thought he was still a boy. And he was scared of me. I began to realize how much of the world I did not know. I was isolated in my little city from everything else.

I was from the city, Lawrence, Kansas, and thought that I knew how to ride and was worldly, but criminal activity was something people just gossiped about. I had never been in a place like this or with people like this. It was invigorating, fascinating, so beautiful, but also so primitive and scary. There was something wonderful about the roughness of the people, their abhorrence of the niceties of city life, and their refusal to follow society's conventions. I loved the freedom of it and not worrying about "being a lady". At the ranch, I could be whatever I wanted and ideally just spend my time riding horses and writing; a perfect combination.

Maxwell Struthers Burt owned the ranch. He wrote amazing short stories such as "Chance Encounters." I soon discovered that they were dedicated to my second cousin, Walter Gilkyson, who owned shares in the ranch. (I guess that is how I got this summer job.) Maxwell Struthers Burt, originally from Philadelphia and a graduate of Princeton, designed the ranch in what would come to be called "Ranch Vernacular." He and his wife were writers, and they were very close to Gilkysin. Many others owned shares in the ranch, and they were writers as well.[2] The ranch was one of the first to be set up for tourists, but the focus was on writing and riding and nature. It was a great place for a young aspiring journalist. The early guests read like a social register and included well-known writers, but also Francis Biddle (later Attorney General under FDR and involved in the WPA). The people who

---

[2] World War 1 gave a boost to the ranch when in 1917 Americans were restricted from travelling outside of the country. But they also wanted the ranch to be a place for advocates of preserving the openness of the land.

worked there included older cowhands and young aspiring writers like me.

I could not wait to meet all of these accomplished writers: Henry Van Dyke who goes there a lot a long with Tucker Rishpam who also owned in on the Ranch, and the Countessa Gizeka, who owned a neighboring ranch but spent most of her time here. She wrote a great many short stories, but I had never heard of most of them. Some have compared the gathering of writers at the Jackson Hole ranch in Wyoming to the Gertrude Stein coterie of artists and writers in Paris. I was determined that I would get to Paris, where I could be with writers and artists as well. Many writers also came to hunt and fish. Even Ernest Hemingway came to the ranch while writing *Farewell to Arms*. Called by some as the Old West, it also attracted artists such as Frederic Remington and photographer William Henry Jackson. Although many also crossed the pond to Europe, they gladly rode with the cowboys and sat around a campfire under the stars, telling stories. Mr. Burt gave me books to read and then quizzed me on them, asking me to tell him what I thought. He told me that he was analyzing me to use as a character for his new book, about a girl who starts in Kansas and begins by being fed up with reform until she finds a sanctuary in nature. Perhaps that is my life.

There were more than 30 cabins, amongst the ponds, barns, sheds, and corrals, with a lodge and dining hall as the central focus. We were so far away from everything that we could have been anywhere. The ranch was located on the west side of the Snake River, in the shadows of the Great Tetons. In 1923, just as I arrived, Burt met with several other like-minded people to fight for the establishment of the Grand Tetons National Park, and to put it under Federal protection. Many a night, there would be discussions about how they might fight against rampant housing developments and industry and preserve the wilderness environment.[3]

It was quiet and peaceful there, and sometimes even boring, but when you put together a group of young people in the wilderness, they will certainly find ways to entertain themselves. We often played tricks on each other. One night, a group of people who had been there for a couple of years before me decided to hold a kangaroo court with charges against the city girl, me. The first charge was that I had alienated the affections of Rex from Anna Van Luyen. I defended myself and replied that the charge was absurd because how could a girl take a man away from a girl

---

[3] The ranch would later become a part of The National Park system.

if he was not willing. Those charges were dropped, but the second was seen as much more serious. I had dared to serve hotcakes to two of the cowpunchers (who I did not like) without syrup. The judge gave me a severe sentence, and I was condemned to ride Chicita, supposedly the wildest horse on the ranch. I was nervous about it, and thought that I would simply refuse, although it would be impossible to live with them if they thought I was scared. Suddenly, when no one was looking, Joe LePage, the cross-eyed, good-hearted foreman, snuck over to me and told me that Chicita can be fine. She reared a little when you first mount her, and then stampedes, but if you let her just run for about two miles, she would tire out, and then you could easily make her behave. Ok, I thought, I can do 2 miles of running. I nodded a thank you to him. The lesson was perseverance.

But I also wanted revenge and hatched a scheme with my new friend Betty (one of the few other girls working at the ranch who was not a native of the area). I acted terrified when they brought Chicita over as I tried to look like a scared little city girl. At first, I worried that my plan would not work. When I got on Chicita, she first snorted and seemed lovely. But as soon as they let go of her head, she simply tore out of there. I quickly adjusted to her rhythm, and it was suddenly so much fun to be flying through the woods, at a marvelous fast gallop. We galloped for about three miles, and by then she was hot and sweaty, so she calmed down, and was easy to control.

We rode about 5 more miles to the JY Ranch (a ranch that Burt had originally been a partner in). I got off Chicita, and tied her to a tree under the Aspens, out of sight from everyone at JY. I told them about what happened and my plan to get back at them. They were all for it. We had lunch, walked around, told stories, and laughed for a few hours until we heard a car pull up. They all hid me, as I heard the man ask if I'd passed by on Chicita. "No, we haven't seen anyone or the horse," they replied. I stayed there until about 10 o'clock that night. When I saw that everything was winding down and I was getting tired. I figured that I had waited long enough. The wind had started to pick up, and it was obvious that a storm was coming. Meanwhile, back at my ranch, Betty, as planned, began to act hysterical and was put in her bunk to lie down, forcing the girls who had started all of this to do our work at the ranch for the day. At about 9:00 at night, they sent out a search party. But they didn't follow the main road because the car had gone that way earlier in the day. Everyone was getting frantic about what could have happened to me. A little later, at about 9:30 that evening, Thau happened to come by the ranch. When Betty heard him cussing all of them out, she managed to slip out of her bunk and pulled him to the side. She told him our scheme and told him to just follow the main road and to keep quiet about it, and he would find me.

It was really dark by then, but I had always heard that a horse can find its way home in the dark, so I gave Chicita her head and let her take us home. I did tell her to hurry because the storm was getting worse and the clouds all blackened. It soon began to rain, and then quickly turned to snow. Halfway home, I was freezing, and the ground was covered in white. I was now getting upset and scared, becoming more and more nervous, wondering if perhaps I had gone too far and done this to myself. Then, I suddenly heard a horse coming full speed toward me. As the lone rider approached me at nearly midnight, I wished that I had learned to shoot a gun. He jumped down and muttered, 'crazy girl.' I was so glad to see it was Thau, and to also see that Thau was not dead, arrested, or had he killed the sheriff. He gave me a blanket and told me to put his chaps on. We tore home the rest of the way. I stumbled from my horse while Thau, being such a good sport, told them that he miraculously found me in the woods, crying, cold, and lost. Everyone was so contrite and did everything for me. It wasn't any trouble to have chills, to cry, and secretly laugh as they brought me food, beer and hot water bottles, and blankets.[4]

---

[4] Tuesday June 20 (1923)

Most days were not as exciting. Amongst the endless mosquitoes and heat, the boredom again started to settle in. There was no communication with the outside world, and rarely did we even see a newspaper. I tried to write most days, after taking care of the horses, but quickly reverted to pranks for immediate satisfaction. One female guest, scheduled for the whole summer, was always yelling at everyone and treating us as if we were mind readers and should know what she wanted. She was especially rude to the chambermaids, so Betty and I hatched a plan with the chambermaids. We put mice and snakes in her room. At least the snakes would have a nice meal. I guess I did always hanker after a Huck Finn life. So, I was thrilled when, on a Sunday, my day off, Jack, who was a guest, asked me to go with him to a friend's ranch 16 miles away. It was a beautiful ride past two lakes, and what would soon be a winter wonderland scene. It was glorious to see new faces and have a ride longer than the usual 6 or 7 miles with the guests. When we arrived, there was a piano in their lodge, and Thau was there. Thau sang to me, trying to get my attention away from Jack and the two other boys from Yale and Williams College. The boy from Williams College, Steve, fascinated me as he told me about the Berkshires of Western Massachusetts. He spoke of the beautiful mountains and lakes, the changing seasons, and the beauty of the Fall season. He said that it never gets very hot, nor very cold, at least compared to Wyoming. It is midway between

Boston and New York City, so it seemed like a perfect place to go if I ever got away from Kansas. I always wanted to go to the big cities, see museums, hear music, go to plays, but I also loved the mountains and woods that I saw here in Wyoming. It seemed like an ideal place to live. I would keep it in my mind for more than a decade before I finally got there and met Charlie Phelps of Otis. I was happy that I would see Steve again, when a couple of weeks later, he invited me to go to Tony's ranch with Betty. We couldn't head over there until work was over at 7:30 PM. We had been riding for an hour, and were coming around by Timber Island when two of the college boys popped out of the darkness to lead us on a shortcut through the moonlit pines. I laughed and was reminded of the scene in *The Emperor Jones*, where he was lost. The night air was crisp and smelled like balsa wood. When we got there, Steve sat by a small fire, all alone. He seemed so peaceful and far away. They made us a wonderful dinner. I was so impressed because it was all cooked by the men, and they later sang to us as they played a guitar. Is this the way the men on the East Coast act? Certainly, the men that I knew in Kansas would never do this! We stayed until 3:00 AM, warmed by the fire. Then the boys accompanied us back to our ranch. The ride home was even better, with little fog clouds caught in the mountains. The stars twinkled through as the clouds moved, and the tops of the mountains were covered by the fog. It was such a peaceful, happy time, without a care in the world.

We were one of the only girls working at the ranch, so several of the young men were always trying to get our attention. Betty and I had become so close that she was like family now, and I sympathized with her as one cowpuncher, Joe, kept trying to capture her affections. Joe was the type of Westerner who had two sides to his nature. One was attractive, picturesque, and rather lovable, and the other was childish and mean. He was the kind who showed his mean side when he didn't get his way. It was always interesting to observe the nature of men when they want someone whom they cannot get, and that they are obviously not very good at pursuing. Joe was desperate. He thought that he would win Betty over by offering her a horse. For a week, she declined his offer. Finally, she asked him if he meant it as a gift or an obligation. He said gift, so she let him put her brand on the horse and named him Jet. He kept telling her of his love for her and said, "Now you don't have to make up your mind. Just be thinking of it all summer and then tell me before it's time for you to go." Betty said that she came to the ranch so that she didn't have to think. He started to get more persistent and then questioned why I was always around Betty. Betty told him that she wouldn't go anywhere without me. Finally, Betty was so annoyed by his constant bothering and being so pushy that she finally lost all her sweetness and told him off. Joe was just nasty after that to everyone. Next thing we knew, Betty's horse, the "gift", was lost. Bill, the wrangler in charge of the horses, claimed that it must have gone off with the others and then wandered away. When we went to the corral, we saw that the others were all there. We told Joe, and then Joe yelled at Bill, but in such a way that we knew it was fake. Any self-respecting cowboy would have pulled a gun if they thought that their horse was taken, but he didn't and didn't seem to care much. On the third day, we took a walk to the river and saw hoof prints of a shod horse, so it couldn't be a wild horse. We followed the hoof prints until we came to the river and saw Jet, a 16-hand beautiful black horse with a long mane. He was standing with Cutie, a Chestnut brown quarter horse, and her colt. He had no saddle or reins and wouldn't leave his family. They were all just a quarter mile from the ranch. When I got back, I simply asked Bill if he had looked by the river. He said yes every day. We decided that we would have to figure out how to get Jet back to the ranch despite Joe and Bill. We thought that if we got a bucket of oats, some rope, and a hackamore to put on him, we could lead him back to the ranch. At night, we snuck into the barn, and we were ready to go when we turned around and bumped into Struthers. We told him that we were off on a great adventure but needed his help. He made us promise not to get shot and to call him if we got into a tight spot. We slowly approached Jet the next day, keeping our distance as we offered the oats. We tried to get the rope around his neck, but he would just run off. We decided that we needed Struthers. Betty sat dejected by the riverbank, keeping a watchful but downturned eye on Jet, holding out her hat filled with oats, and her other hand with the hackamore. Meanwhile, I ran back as quickly as I possibly could to get Struthers. He quietly snuck away from the ranch with a rope in hand, and once out of sight, ran after me to the river. He had no problem securing the horse, so we went back a different way and out of sight after we gave the lead to Betty. Betty walked back to the corral just as the roughnecks gathered round. She just walked arrogantly in with Jet on a rope. Everyone looked at Bill, who said that he couldn't find the horse. They laughed at him and praised the little city girl for being so capable. She certainly made him look bad. So much for it being a gift. Joe was as cross as a bear and was not giving the horse to Betty if she did not return his affections. [5] Struthers never said a word, although he said that it was a story that might end up in one of his short stories. And it did.

Struthers Burt (who was finishing "The Diary of a Dude Wrangler" for Saturday Evening Post), Van Dyck, and Mrs. Rollins (author of the *Cowboy*) were the best part of the summer at

---

[5] August 23, 1923

the ranch. They wanted to know what I thought and told me that my ideas had value. They treated me as an intelligent equal, saw me as a bit wild, but like the horses here, I could be wild but beautiful, elegant, and comforting. I could be tamed, although they warned me not to get too tame! One day Henry Van Dyke came up to Betty and me and said, "Now this afternoon, I want to talk with you two youngsters." He sat with us and asked us what we were planning to do, and then, gradually, this kind old man took our hand and came to the point. "Please don't get married until you've spent at least five years seeing the world. … at least give me five." We explained that we had no prospects or jobs and wanted school and were not interested in glamour. After five years, you'll be ready to consider matrimony, Henry. He also noted that a man should not get married until he is at least 30. By then, a man knows which way he is going. He then told us to stay close to each other, that a good friend makes all the difference. How do you say no to such a sweet old man? I thought that his advice was perfect, although I wanted to write and not ever get married. So much for those plans.

I really wanted to stay in the woods and the mountains forever, or find a place where I could sit in the woods, dangle my feet in a lake, and ride horses. Someday, I may lose myself to the world that I have known. It may become necessary for my peace of mind. I think most clearly when the mountains and moonlight are cold, or when I can see my reflection in the lake. [6]

I wanted to be like Chicita, a little bit difficult unless you gave me my freedom. I wanted to follow Van Dyck's advice and find a way to see the world and stay unattached. I wrote many poems while there, such as:

In the grey woods of my mind —

And other days they drift and shine —

Such free and flying things

I find the gold dust in my hair

Left by their brushing wings[7].

I wrote these words about the freedom of spirit that I felt at the ranch when I was in Wyoming for the summer. I did not want to just give in to a man's wishes, but what other options did I have? While a sense of independence raced through my blood, I heard stories of fairytales, knights in shining armor, and the goal of being that fairy princess. How can I be in that fairy tale if I ride off on a

---

[6] Uncle Charlie and Aunt Nell never had children and would want to educate me in a more proper way. They always spoke of adopting me. He was a Quaker and has many similar ideas to me. I never thought much about religion but there was something about the Quakers and their ideas that I really liked. Uncle Charlie is now also very ill and lonely so Mother told them that they "could have the little faerie in their home". Mother told me that she could give me to them for a year. Was I being discarded or was this a good thing. I am not sure.
[7] Sue Moody letter, 1923

horse all by myself? Do I need a knight or a Prince by my side? I had dismissed Thau and anyone else who said that they would save me.

Even my grandfather wrote of the knights in shining armor and fairy princesses. He became a famous writer of poems about Kansas, including a book-length poem, and non-fiction. After having fought in the Civil War for the North, he became a politician and was elected to office. He was a noted abolitionist and, early on, fought for women's rights. His activist spirit, I believe, was in my blood, and yet he also wrote about Lawrence, Kansas, and protecting the women there. He wrote:

"Of valor, who shall question that?

Each one and night, I kissed the hand

Lady love, and sworn to stand

by honest sword in foreign land,

swore by the spurs, and tipped the hat.

Husbands and wives, and little ones,

kings and queens on Kansas soil,

slash their empire rest secure from broil

in here and peaceful life the toil,

slash and raise for liberty her sons.

Sweet Lawrence! Freedoms child!

Cradled in love and taught them the mild

and gentle ways of truth, she smiled

in graceful beauty not unseen…

The love of men for men she taught;

she taught that human rights are dear;

she loved the home, and sought to cheer

 sad heart: and she directed here

a citadel for honest thought.

I felt like I was two people and had to reconcile who I wanted to be. I wanted to be like my grandfather, but I was a girl. I loved the me that had been working at a ranch, mostly with men, and loved that most of the time they treated me as an equal. I wanted to feel like an equal. At the ranch, I got to ride all the time, but also got to write every day. It was a place in the wilderness that was a true writer's colony. Most of the men, and even some women there had been published.

Now, I was in the middle of a war in Paris, and far from home. How etiquette completely changes during bombardments. When sirens wailed, we ran for our lives. We went into the large "cave" that was the basement of our building, or ran into the trenches in the woods, or sometimes, exhausted, weak, and hungry, we just lay in our bed and prayed. During the first days of the Bombardments, I was in Paris near the Galeries Lafayette when a huge "messerschmidt" flew overhead. A little man in blue grabbed my arm quickly and hurried me to a Metro tunnel. Later, I discovered that he was a French marine officer, so he recognized the plane as German before the sirens even went off.

I thought that perhaps by going back to Paris as a journalist during an impending war, I could rediscover my Chicita spirit. But now that I was here, I had to realize that I was totally on my own. There was no knight in shining armor, or a sombrero, when I needed it the most, maybe there never was. Perhaps, I just had to find my way to save myself. Certainly, no one was coming to save us, and we had to be happy for whatever little help at survival we could find.

Chapter 3
Opal

When Johnny and I first went to Paris in 1927, I decided to keep a journal, and I wrote in it every day. Now I scrounged through my desk in the apartment to find it. I knew that I had brought it with me on the ship because I wanted to show Bobby my Paris and revisit my favorite restaurants. I tried to describe the many pictures in my mind of Paris, from the long, lovely vistas of the interiors of the galleries, just one masterpiece after another. It is easy to understand why it has always been a city full of artists and writers, and why artists are happy living on just a crust of bread. Paris was like walking on clouds. It is, or was, the city of beauty.

Paris spoils you for living anywhere else in the world. Especially in Paris, I always wanted to find the right hat and handbag. Fashion was so important here. There is such a 'live and let live' spirit. Many Parisians are bad, many are dirty, many are lazy, many are in love with one thing, many with another. And yet they live in their district where there are more people like them. Johnny and I had gone all over, and no one made us try to be like one of them. And they never hurry, just live, and take your time doing whatever it is you want to do. All I wanted to do was stroll the streets, shops, galleries, and write.

We sat together on the right side of the Jeanne D'Arc sculpture. (Now it was the meeting place of those anxious about war.) She sits majestically on the horse, waving her flag in the center of Paris. Gilded and triumphant, she rises from where she was wounded at the Place de Pyramides. A woman respected for her gallantry, perseverance, and fortitude, Jean D'Arc is a symbol for Paris, perhaps for all women. As if emphasizing her endless power, behind her, were a series of arches which melted into one another in a series of dim shadows. They led one into another until your eyes were lost in the vague promises of what lay beyond. Looking up, following the glorious, aspiring arches, I was lost at the time, in the beyond, and what my future held. I was at the beginning of my career, my life, and it seemed as if there were endless possibilities for love, family, and above all, a career. It was like a religious experience. Paris captured the spirit of worship. The soaring cathedrals, the lines of Chartres, lines leading you up to the roof, which is more magnificent in breadth than the vaulting. Flying buttresses and gargoyles watch over the city. No wonder the first Napoleon said, "How ill at ease an atheist would feel in this place!"

When Johnny and I went to Notre Dame Cathedral and we climbed up the dark, winding stone stairs of the left tower. If we spent a hundred days in succession looking for the most elegiac experience, we would never again find a day like this one. Looking out over the whole city, we saw white fluffy clouds hanging over the Seine as it wound its way under all the bridges like a narrow silvery ribbon. Gradually, it grew darker and darker, until we noticed spray-like sheets of rain spread like gauzy sails and drifting over the right bank with the wind. Suddenly, the rain was pouring down on us, and the wind was puffing with all its strength, to blow us off the turret of Notre Dame and send us like parachutes over Paris. It was such fun to hold onto the 800-year-old balustrade of the very tippy top of that tower. I wondered whether it would suddenly crumble and melt in the water, watching it spout forth in great torrents from the mouths of the sassy gargoyles. The gargoyles are so fascinating. There is one who conscientiously looks over Paris all day and night. With his chin in his hands, his elbows rested on the balustrade, and his tongue stuck out. He looked bored from listening to the gargoyle next to him, who seemed to continuously laugh and tell raucous stories. They are odd creatures to be sitting on the top of a cathedral. But they have the most wonderful view of Paris and never have to come down. I wanted to just stay there with them forever, relishing these moments with Johnny and Paris.

Were the gargoyles still keeping an eye on Paris, or would they also be destroyed?

The trains held endless adventures for us, and we kept trying to see more and more of France. We went to the train station and decided to take a train to Chantilly, but it was the day before pay day and we had hardly any money. We decided to go third class. Just across from us was a very friendly Frenchman with one leg. He and Johnny gave each other one look, and they were off back in World War I, supposedly the war to end all wars. The whole way to Chantilly, they fought the war again and presented stories to one another, all in French. Do soldiers have a private sign?

As they relived the war, I remembered how one day a trumpeter squad had passed beneath our window in Paris playing a patriotic march. They celebrated that an armistice for World War I had been signed, and there would never be another world war. How naive. I wrote in my journal that day, "Wars are terrible and always, I suppose, only the women will deplore them because men seem to enjoy a fight now and then. Only when they become too cruel and face the destructive gases and horrible tortures will the world of men maybe become pacifists. You must know that all our fellow men need to learn to love each other, and the water and the air. "

When we left the train, the whole third-class carriage yelled out *au revoir*.

When you get off the train in Chantilly, you plunge into the forest with trees like you have never seen. They are thousands of years old and trimmed with dark green velvet moss. The trees themselves have a russet-brick cast to them. We followed an old stone wall covered with vines for miles. After walking through the forest, we ate our supper on a stone bench surrounded by four giant oaks. From where we sat, we could see the Chateau that belonged to a Prince. It is a grey palace surrounded by a moat and reached by a beautiful bridge and green gate with two great green hanging lamps.

We returned to Paris relaxed and exhilarated, when suddenly we opened our door and realized that our apartment had been broken into. It was very strange because, since we had moved there, the place had not been empty for long periods. We racked our brains to think of who might have known we would be gone for an extended time. We thought that it was a very safe place. At 9 o'clock, the concierge locked the big door. When we entered after that time, we had to ring the bell until she woke up, pressed us in, and unbolted the door. Someone could have entered and known that they would not be disturbed unless the bell rang downstairs. Everything was in disarray, and we began to look for what was missing. I was so upset and felt really violated when I realized what was missing. It was the pretty pink panties with pink lace ruffles that my mother made for me. One of the servants probably thought that I wouldn't miss one piece of silk underwear. I would just think that I had misplaced it. The reason I knew it was missing was because Johnny had been looking for something and had pulled some things out from my drawer and laid them on top. We were distraught, so I changed my shoes and stockings, and we went out for a walk. When we came back, we instituted a search. We took everything out of the wardrobe piece by piece and shook it. I even took all my dresses off the hangers, we looked under the bed, in the bed, and under the bathtub. It was gone, there was no doubt about it. When I wash my underwear, I hang it on a line in the bathroom over the tub. No girls had been in this apartment since I washed all three pairs and laid them carefully away. It was simply an unfathomable mystery. My little anniversary ring with sapphires and diamonds was there on top of the mantle in my jewel box, which was next to my big makeup box. It was really very strange. It made me so mad because I loved those panties. It was a rare gift from my mother. I was going to tell the English-speaking proprietor when she came back on Monday, but in the meantime, we were locking everything up in the wardrobe and closet and carrying the keys with us. Who would want my panties anyway, and why? It seemed so important then.

To make me feel better, Johnny suggested that we go for dinner at the *Suckling Pig*, an adorable little place right near the Arc de Triomphe and surrounded by cute little shops. Walking there, I found a notebook in a shop, and then some etchings in another. The outside of the restaurant was all wood-paneled. The inside only had about 10 tables. There were red tile floors, red and white checkered tablecloths, and long red, perfectly upholstered leather benches. To enter, you walked down a few steps to wooden tables and chairs. We sat right in the window and watched all the people at every table talking enthusiastically with their hands. The walls were cream colored with brown panels and had plaques painted with pigs figuring in each scene. Below it, there was an appropriate French verse painted on the wall. It was fun to try to read the verse about the pig.

I remember one rhyme:

A little pig

Hanging from the ceiling

Pull its tail it will lay some eggs.

Pull it harder, it will lay some gold.

The main platter was one of a pig enthroned on a platter, and five chickens below revolving on a spit before the open fire. There were huge brown crocks for butter, and little wicker baskets of strawberries and grapes. Even the dishes were heavy crockery with pigs painted on them, and around the edge were sausages. All this design was done in the same reddish brown as the restaurant. We requested a Bordeaux, which they brought in a little brown jug. Ready to eat our meal, we were not disappointed. The food at the restaurant was divine.

Finally, when Spring arrived, we were off to the Bois de Boulogne and the races. It was simply heavenly! Little black trees blossoming, soft pink or white flowers. It seemed like they were all in their Spring fashion. It wasn't like any woods that I have ever seen. There were so many colors in the trees. Some with long plum branches like ostrich feathers, or pale green; some were mustard colored, while others were bright yellow. The poplars were standing tall and graceful by the lagoon and appeared as a yellow-green in the distance as the road curves. Where but in France could you spend Easter at the races? Mr. Crafton, Johnny, and I all attended the "Prix de President de la Republique". The horse racecourse out in the Bois has a stadium with many towers of cream-colored stone, grilled stairways, glass enclosures, flower boxes, and green trimmings to match the big trees stretching away for acres in the Bois. From high up in the stadium, we saw the towers and spires of the city reaching out for miles. And then the horses below strutted and danced and stretched their glossy, long necks. They seem like beautiful ladies in flowered pussy willows and taffeta, and the colors in the air were intoxicating, as if you were at an elegant costumed ball. Flower petals swirled around our feet. Then, some black and white ducks apparently in formal dress came by. It was now clear to me where the first tailors got their conception for black tie formal wear. Johnny teased one, and they all flew away. Of course, we bet on the horses, but not knowing anything about the horses, we picked them out by the names we liked. Scot's grey Socks was nobody's favorite, but he was the only English horse, so we had to bet on him. And the jockey wore the Union Jack. When he came out, he was literally an old grey mare. He was big and seemed confused as to where he was. The horses started to go, and Grey Socks started to run in the other direction. By the jockey's pure strength and cunning, he got him to turn around. Suddenly, Grey Socks saw the other horses ahead of him and wanted to join the party. He rushed ahead, and when he was next to another horse, he started tossing his head, wanting to play. It didn't seem like he knew that he was in a race. When he reached the first jump, I couldn't watch. We had seen another jockey carried off from a race when the horse failed to clear the jump. Suddenly, it seemed like it penetrated Grey Sock's big, thick skull that he was in a race and had to jump and wanted to win. He suddenly stepped out briskly, took off at an incredible speed, and passed the tape by a nose ahead of all the rest. All the screaming spectators fell back in amazement. A few whooped joyously with us. The jockey jumped off and fell to the ground, and the horse kept running like he was having a good time. The British horse paid us 10 – 1. It took care of all our other losses from the other races. Never doubt one's ability, even if everyone says that it cannot be done.

Johnny and I had tried cafes, restaurants, and Bistros. All the meals were extraordinary. A lunch consisted of *hors d'oeuvres*, mostly cold meats, fish, ham, calves' brains, and morsels of veal. Then the waitress announced that she would bring the meat course, which included chicken, salad, cheese, and bread. Lastly, they served a huge bowl of chocolate mousse for us to share.

On another day, when Johnny had off, we went to an unforgettable French Village Fair. Everyone was drinking wine at the little tables, and the women, old and young, were in provincial costumes. There were puppets in the form of fat, rosy-cheeked men who rolled their eyes and opened their mouths in conversation while a spieler was doing his stuff. Then the real men appeared, fat and rosy-cheeked like the puppets, standing in their Brittany coats and hats, rolling their eyes in the very same way. They each invited girls over to the tables or stalls for something to eat. There were the Gingerbread stalls, the pommes frites stalls and all kinds of side shows of sword swallowers, jugglers and some performance. There were clowns wherever we walked. There was a merry-go-round, and dancing in the street to the constant music.

When winter came again, I longed for those fun-filled warm summer days. I complained like a child. Winter in Paris is very dark, dreary, and rainy. When you get sick, it just seems as if the sun will never poke through. There was nothing really the matter with me except that I got awfully cold and chilled to the bone when I ventured out to the flea market. I had to stay in bed for two days, and Johnny seemed so worried about me. He gently covered me with blankets, brought hot water bottles, and made me eat.

I told Johnny that I think that next winter we will leave Paris and go to the Pyrenees near Spain, but still in France, where we can talk to the natives, breathe in the ocean air, and write all day in the golden sunshine. We will continue to learn French, to speak like a native, and then my ultimate goal is, of course, to write a novel. My world was filled with hopes and dreams.

Johnny got a weekend evening off and told me that he had a big surprise. He knew that the tickets would surely boost my spirits. I couldn't imagine what it was, but when we went into the Salle Gaveau, a few steps from the Champs-Élysées, I knew that it was something extraordinary. I sensed it when I noted all the snooty sophisticated people chatting in the lounge. I suddenly saw on the poster that it was a Paul Robeson concert. I have never seen such a performance, such a display of personality, such a voice. I think that he is descended from a Black King somewhere. Paul Robeson has used his voice, his art, and his brilliance to help others. The world needs more people like Paul Robeson, especially now.

At first, the audience adopted an air of, "I've heard much finer voices than yours, but you've had a great deal of publicity, so I'm here to be bored." When he came out on the stage with the grace and rush that an athlete shows, I just glowed with pride because he was American. There was such charm and refinement and self -effacement about his conduct that you couldn't help but wishing that all your snooty white friends could see this magnificent Negro man. And yet there was a surety about his entire performance that left no doubt in your mind that he was a master. The audience talked, mumbled, and rustled in their seat. Robeson waited a full five minutes for them to get ready to listen to him. No nervousness showed, just a little boredom at their behavior. When the house was finally as quiet as a Mormon Tabernacle, he sang. And how he sang. Such music! It was easy, comfortable – like listening to a friend, and yet there was a boyish sweetness about it. But oh, the power of that voice, while his tones were things to savor. The records don't get it. After the first group of songs, he left the stage in a sort of half-disgusted manner. He didn't like his audience. You could see that. His music was art. It was sincerity. They were hypocritical. They weren't getting it. They applauded politely, and he came back to sing "Water Boy". It would have moved hearts of stone. They just had to go wild over him after that. He had loosened them up. Encore after encore until, when he left the stage at last, they were still stomping and shouting like hoodlums. But Robeson, in granting the encores, in singing their requests, was polite, self-contained, and a real artist in his behavior. Never once did he catch their hoodlum spirit and become one of them. Paul Robeson made the audience look like two cents before he finished with them. At last, he left them clapping until they were worn out. I hated to leave; never was I so proud to be an American in Paris. When I hear a record or radio play of him singing, I am once again filled with that pride.

We felt so comfortable in Paris and were constantly meeting new friends from all over the world. One afternoon, we passed by *Le Chat Noir,* the famous supper club, hours before it opened. It is known for having the most avant-garde music. Artists who live nearby have their work shown on the walls inside. We gave the girl by the door 5 francs, and she let us look inside. There were crayon drawings of Montmartre celebrities on every side of the wall.

Inside, we met this wonderful Russian Princess, Mme. Cranovitch, who grew up with an English governess, so she spoke English perfectly. She was very intelligent, interesting, and wanted to learn all about America. She had very thick hair and coarse lips and was a bit stocky. We shared stories about Russia, Russian writers, French opera, America, everything. She also told me of a woman who would improve my French in exchange for English lessons. Before she was to leave for her travels back home, she invited Johnny and me to come to her house and then invited us to her box at the opera. She became a wonderful new friend, and we often went to the theater and museum together.

One day, she took me around the corner to a little old grey-haired Russian refugee who was an artist. I wanted to buy one of her paintings. She said that I could pay half now and half after I got home, so it would only cost $30. I told her that I would bring Johnny there on Saturday. This began my buying of art. After that, I decided that wherever I travelled, I would try to purchase art. I thought that I had a good eye and could resell these pieces when I got home, selling collectors a little piece of Europe.

Now that I was back in Paris, a decade later, Mme. Cranovitch was one of the few people that was there that I knew. She would come by from time to time, and each time was a very different experience. It was usually very hard for a small boy to have tea with an older person, especially the ladies. Certainly, he did not trouble himself to juggle a teacup or to ask for a second. She had brought a basket, one with a little crock of yellow butter from a farmer she knew, two or three large eggs from another very old and close friend of hers, and three carrots. I had the remainder of a jar of Mirabelles, so we sat down to a feast. Mirabelles are small plums that I had found growing in an abandoned lot and made into a jam. They were sweet, so they tasted good as a jam without much sugar. Bobby liked the idea and certainly found no trouble at all in eating the little bit of bread and butter with a slice of apple that she brought with her.

He was fascinated by her expressions of rage one minute, and by an angel's smile the next. She would recount stories of the British soldier and the obstacles she had to overcome. "And what do you think a soldier is made of?" she asked Bobby point-blank, slashing a huge chunk of butter off and slapping it onto bread, followed by a large spoonful of Maribel jam. "I – – I don't know, "admitted Bobby, "but I guess, muscles he said uneasily." "Muscles." She retorted, "Certainly soldiers are made of muscles, not made of sugar candy, my boy. You would never see one climb in the Alps, skiing over the slopes and tracking across the long plains of Libya if he were with you? Dressed in red and white stripes like the guards standing at Buckingham Palace? I should say you would not. They are made of muscle, and all they need is good food to nourish those muscles."

She looked sadly down at her piece of stale bread, and suddenly she turned to me and said, "What was it we used to drink over there at your house when you were in Paris last time? Wasn't it something called Ovaltine? I wonder if we could find that now in the drug stores when they re-open here. It might be a solution, you know. There will be no more real coffee for the fridge until the end of the war." Now, she wailed softly at me as though she might be reading my thoughts and then fairly whispered the words, "Doesn't it nearly kill you to drink they're filthy substitute? Why doesn't it taste like coffee to me at all? Simply no taste whatsoever. And all during the war, while their armies are marching around, now filled with a French omelette made from Madame Poullard's eggs, stews made from Normandy's chickens. She was looking at my red face with dismay, "And whatever the matter is with you, come over here and sit down." I excused myself and went to the kitchen. Everyone knew it was an impossibly rude thing, unthinkable to actually take a little old lady's scarf and choke her with it so that she could not talk. Although my hands were itching to do just that, of course, I could not. I was a grown lady, I was Bobby's mother. I rose quickly, and to my dismay, it seemed to me that I would certainly snatch the scarf from this old lady's throat. I would have to strangle her with it if she continued to yell every moment against Hitler in every way. Her voice carried loudly out the window for the German soldiers to hear. She was like a music box that got wound up and couldn't stop standing on the street.

The tea kettle was singing, and I let it continue to drown out her voice. She could land us all in prison. So, I stood there listening to the tea kettle and wondering how I could get her up to realize that this was really Hitler's country now. He had conquered it. It was really very dangerous for her to be talking about him that way. Not only treacherous for her, but unsafe for all of us, for the French people she knew and talked to who could be so easily excited, as French people often are. Or it could be very dangerous for every single person in this land if we all began to talk about Hitler, it might throw us into prison, or worse.

It was also very sad thinking of what we had been through and what was coming next. We heard that the Germans intended to bombard London with their airplanes, ships, and submarines, to capture London or else to make as much trouble as they could.

We also heard that they were thinking of marching into Russia and getting Italy to join them, to conquer the whole of Europe. Would we ever have anything to really eat again, any enjoyment, any sense of peace and comfort in life?

In the middle of my sad thoughts came the sound of a funny little cackling boy singing. I hurried into catch what Bobby's laughter was about. Madame Cranovitch was standing in the middle of the room with a hat like a crown so straight around the head that it made it look like a lid starting to top off the tea pot, her little nose was pointing forward and she was pointing toward it then turning to wave her coat tails as she sang the little song.

"I'm a little teapot,

short and stout,

here is my handle (her coat tails)

here's my spout (her nose)

when I get excited sing and shout

just pick me up,

and pour me out."

It was raining outside, and she seemed terribly excited. Now she sang the verse a second time and left out part of the words and put whistles and Gobbels in like this pour me out (she did the "pour me out" exactly like water running out of the fat nozzle of some very old teapot or like the rain for the mouth of the gargoyles by Notre Dame. We all laughed like we had not in a long time. Bobby shouted and wanted her to sing so that he could catch the gurgling sound one more time.

> I'm a little teapot
>
> short and (snort)
>
> here is my whistle
>
> here's my spout (whistle)
>
> when I get excited
>
> sing and shout just me pick me up
>
> and (gurgle, gurgle, gurgle)

Now she refused to help herself to several lumps of sugar which happened to linger at the bottom of my sugar bowl as if there was no problem getting more tomorrow. We are all on strict rations and restrictions, but she didn't care. I didn't know how we would ever happen to put any more sugar in the sugar pot. "Madame," she said, "did you ever hear the second verse?" "No," I admitted, and I only remembered vaguely hearing the first one. "Well, here it is." She spread her skirts with a little flutter and put the lid noticeably onto the sugar bowl.

> "I'm the bowl for sugar
>
> I'm short too,

if it weren't for you I 'd have

  grew and grew

  just remove my hat (she took the lid off with great flourish)

  and take a peek 'n lo

sugar is sweet, and so are you."

She handed Bobby a lump of sugar, and we proceeded to drink a watered-down tea

"Hey," cried Bobby suddenly what about the cream pitcher, "doesn't that have a verse? "

She disregarded him and continued to talk to me in a low but audible voice about all the wrongs that Hitler and his men were inflicting. Of course, I wouldn't want Bobby to hear this and repeat it, she said, but they are even thinking of…."

Bobby interrupted, "Isn't there one about the cream picture?" I said, "He might repeat it on the street to some of his friends." She whispered, "You know little tickle-pitchers have big ears." "What?" Bobby asked. Surprised, she turned and shouted at him, "I said little pitchers have big ears, and so have you." "What does that mean?" Bobby asked blankly."It means that when two grown-ups are talking a in low tone so that you won't hear them, you are sure to cock your ears and hear everything even if it's a whisper. And wait a minute, don't interrupt. Then you were sure to run and tell." "No, I won't," said Bobby with his big eyes. "I won't tell. I won't tell." She was screaming at him again. "We were talking about Hitler." "Well, what of it?" "I don't know, I didn't hear anything." "Yes, you can't tell, that's splendid, then well, since you're such a good boy and never listen to a grown-up saying things in private, I will give you the third verse!"

> "I'm the tickle picture (she held the cream pot)
> high short and fat
> right by the side of the pot
> I sat
> when I saw him spouting
> laughed for glee
> that's because you're fat
> you see

It was wonderful to have her and all her eccentricities. She made us laugh, live, and cry. But another time, Madame Cranovitch came from Paris one day in a rage. "I saw the most horrible thing just now on the street. It was a poster that completely covered a wall. It was a huge gross notice. A command." I begged her to tell me what it looked like. She explained how there was a big picture of a German soldier, just like the ones passing by your house. She waved toward the window with disdain as her voice dropped to almost a whisper. We knew that the worst was coming. "He was carrying in his arms… a little French child! The poster told French children that if they needed anything or saw anything, go talk to a German soldier!" "Bobby, is that what you should do? Run up to the first German soldier you see if you happen to be having a little trouble about something? Shout Heil Hitler!!" "NEVER!" Bobby was a small boy, and he still didn't understand not to speak to anyone on the street about the horrors of Hitler. I begged him to stop, especially after it was learned that 4 French boys were killed while demonstrating against Hitler at the Arc de Triomphe. Anyone, even a young boy, would be shot if they wore a tri-color band on their arm.

But Bobby developed his own opinions listening to the grown-ups' talk. Usually, the soldiers ignored Bobby, but one day, as 7 or 8 boys surrounded him as he discussed the horrors of war and Hitler, one German soldier had had enough. They went straight up to Bobby as the other boys ran off. He stared at Bobby and said, "Enough" in a very stern voice. Bobby just looked down at the ground and didn't say a word. The silence was oppressive. The German officer then turned to Bobby and gave him a piece of chocolate as long as he never said another word about Hitler. Then the soldier told Bobby that if he did say anything about Hitler that his mother would be taken away and put in a concentration camp. Months went by with Bobby not mentioning Hitler. The German soldier saved his life by sufficiently terrifying him.

Chapter 4
Red Beads

In September 1929, Johnny and I returned to NYC from Paris, full of hope and promise for our new life together. So, we returned to Boston and then took a train to New York on September 21. In looking for a job for myself, I forgot about Paris for a bit when I was offered a job in NYC. I was given a job as soon as I arrived, as long as I had two articles to hand in once I arrived: one on Paris styles, and one on French cooking. But before we could leave, I had an appendicitis attack while in Paris. I realized that I had these problems for years, but now they took it out at the American hospital in Paris, so I had no time to write the two articles. I was determined to write it on the boat back to NYC.

My fantasy world of Paris and being a writer would end abruptly. It seems that the realities of life always interrupt our fantasies. Life to come was foreshadowed by our Equity ship fellow passenger, HG Wells. Wells had carried on non-stop, that after the Titanic sank 17 years earlier, our ship would not make it back! That everyone on the ship was doomed to sink. Our ship did not sink physically, but our lives and spirits would within weeks of our landing back in the U.S. Just one month later, on a Thursday in October of 1929, the stock market crashed, and the world economic ship sank. We returned from Paris in 1929 after our wonderful trip abroad. Johnny wrote, I took French lessons and strolled the streets of the most beautiful city in the world, to what soon turned into a very different America. An America of homelessness, breadlines, and depression. Columnist Will Rogers would write the following Tuesday that people were "waiting online to find a window to jump out of." The city and papers were filled with stories of men turning the gas on in their homes to kill themselves because they could not deal with the losses. The super wealthy at first thought that it was just a slight nuisance, but they too soon suffered, and the lavish parties became less frequent and less lavish, or not at all.

Within a month of our return, the stock market crashed, and although I had no money in the stock market, it impacted every aspect of the economy.

By 1930, 25% of America's workforce was unemployed. At the worst point, one-third of New Yorkers were unemployed, and Central Park became a Hooverville, a place for the homeless to sleep, pitch a makeshift tent, and try to find some food. The farmers of 1929 had a bumper crop of apples, and homeless men walked the NYC streets selling apples. By 1934, there were 75,000 single, destitute homeless women in NYC. The women had nothing to sell except sometimes their bodies; they stayed 5 in a flop house, if they could, or rode the subways all night long.

Despite all the advances for women's rights just a few years earlier, everyone now believed that women should relinquish their jobs, stay home with the children, and let the men have the few jobs that were available so that they could support their families. In a poll, more than 80% of Americans again believed that a woman's place was in their home. In 1932, twenty-six states made it illegal for a married woman to work! In the winter of 1932-33, faced with bread lines and Hoovervilles, single unemployed women marched in NYC streets demanding jobs. The optimism of the 1920s and promises of Franklin Delano Roosevelt had been wiped out just as much as the bank accounts of more prosperous families. Women with a good college education and a degree from the Katherine Gibbs School might get a secretarial job. Women in Journalism expanded in the 1920s, and Eleanor Roosevelt held press conferences for women only.

I thought that the depression in America was the worst thing that I could have experienced. Having become Sue Moody White, a married lady, I thought that I had everything. I had travelled in France and Italy, met with important people, other writers, and could now figure out the balancing act. I had returned from our trip to Paris determined to write. I would look to feminist icons, other women writers, and men who had been mentors, and yet it all seemed nearly impossible. I arrived home from Paris with my first article in hand for the *NY Herald Tribune*. They asked for an article about food. That launched me into a series that would help pay some bills and keep me writing. Women journalists generally did not get the more serious assignments, like war and politics, but I could turn a recipe into an essay.

Or, as one publisher wrote, "so you want to be a reporter," and continued to tell it like it was: "in the films you have seen, they have women who find work as reporters and go on to break the big story. Fairy dust, ladies. …if you imagine in your dreams that it'll be you covering the presidential conference, take a good deep breath and remember that you are a Susie Susie? Did I mention Susie, all the gang called the new female recruits Susie until they do something outstanding and earn a different name."[8] At the same time, places like the Barbizon hotel and women's magazines told women that if they wanted to get ahead with their career, they had to not be a slave to domesticity, husbands, children, and dinner parties. The models and the career women all wore hats, a sign that you were a career woman and not a mother. I had hats from Paris, but now I was also visibly pregnant, and no one would

---

[8] Barbizon Hotel p 59

hire a pregnant married woman, even if I had a great hat from Paris.

I was so upset, distraught, frazzled, and frightened by then, and just thought that I would get lost looking for jobs, go into labor, and would surely have the baby in a subway. I couldn't find a good doctor, even. All the doctors said the beds were full and the private hospitals were much too expensive for us. Every time I went to a publisher, all they did was ask me about the baby and when I was due. I managed to get a few articles published at the very beginning, before I was really showing, one with the *Christian Science Monitor*. It is a publication on sale in Kansas, Nebraska, Georgia, New Jersey, and on all the better newsstands. They've been very cordial and will probably take some more articles. But other than that, I have not seen a check. Nothing was getting published; things were so bad that the publishers told me that they were using what they had. Everyone was suffering, not just New York magazines. I was told that the *Saturday Evening Post* was interested in something that I wrote, but so far, nothing. I went to the *Herald Tribune* magazine, nothing now. And there was a woman at McMillan's interested in a book I was doing; she should let me know pretty soon, and if she didn't, then someone at Doubleday was also interested. I had a novel all finished, ready to go over, and I sent it to an editor in Philadelphia. After the glory of Paris, life was so depressing; nothing was happening.

Soon after, I returned to New York, I wrote to my father that we were about down to zero, financially. Long ago ran out of money, and we were now running out of creditors and bankers. What shall we do? Bobby was so sweet, and I wanted to provide for him, but how could I? All our other friends were in the same predicament. The problem was especially delicate in the fact that journalists never had any money, and most of our friends were journalists. Other journalists similarly could not get in to see anyone. Mrs. Laurents said that she tried to borrow $500 on a mortgage-free building worth $40,000 and could not get anything. Publishing houses collapsed, and magazines shrank, so there was suddenly less chance for positions for either of us.

Life was still in the throes of the depression. So many people were still out of work and didn't know which way to turn. It seemed like so many people didn't even care. Could I write about inexpensive ways to cook and decorate, and make people happy with their lives, even if for just a few minutes? It seemed like such a slow and painful climb out of this. Meanwhile, I tried to balance it all.

The dust bowls exacerbated an already difficult situation, and in the plains of the Midwest, farms were wiped out, crops died, and the feeding of livestock was impossible. Johnny's father, who was Vice President of an important university, was laid off along with 10 other faculty members. No one was left untouched by the financial and mental Depression. The farmers out in Kansas, back home, were truly desperate by now. My parents did not have a farm in Kansas, but had apartments in which tenants could no longer afford to pay the rent. My mom and dad were in dire financial shape, and the stress was too much for my dad. In 1936, he had a fatal heart attack, and things went from bad to worse for my mother. There was no way for us to help. After Paris, as we had settled into NYC, we barely had enough to live on and had no money to go and see family.

Bobby had arrived; a joy and a chore. No one ever tells you how much work a child is and how difficult it is to have a child and work, especially when you have no money and it is in the middle of a depression.

I decided to write an article about a baby.

Johnny now worked evenings for the paper, and I had to make a sandwich at night for Johnny to take to work, but the baby was up at 2 and then at 7 am. Got Bobby ready for breakfast, 8:30,

Johnny came home from work, 9:00, I did the dishes, 10:00, took Bobby out in the buggy. Carried him and the buggy down the steps, returned at 11:00, got ready to work, but Bobby fell and was crying, waking up Johnny, who was now yelling for some sleep. I held Bobby and tried to console him, but then the bread man stopped by, and I needed to make everyone lunch. Bobby would soon take a nap, and I would write, so I think! I hadn't washed my hair. Now was my chance. The vegetable man stopped by. Please, just one or two pages. But I cleaned up, Bobby woke up. He played while I would write, maybe. Johnny would be up soon, and I needed to cook for him, do housework, and do laundry. 4:00, snack for Bobby, meal for Johnny, 5:30, make dinner, bathe Bobby. 7:00 Bobby was getting sleepy, so I read to him and put him to bed. I wrote a little song for my Bobby.

> *"Little soft blanket for little soft head*
> *Bobby mustn't cry make his eyes red*
> *Little soft blanket dear little head*
> *pillows at feet and go to bed."*

Next, I gave some time to listen to Johnny talk about work as he got ready. So maybe I could get a couple of hours of writing in the evening, but I was so exhausted, I never seemed to get it done. I wrote best in the morning, but that was just impossible. And yet people said to me, "So, nice that you can follow your career at home and don't have to go out to do your business!" Oh, how I longed for the chance to go out to a place to work, where all I focused on was my work. Let someone else do the housework, even the cooking. Oh, just a chance to write like a business, where I could get my thoughts on paper, into circulation, instead of churning around in my head while I did housework badly. I had this Cinderella-themed story in my head. Show historical interpretation through this modern idea, weaving Cinderella and Bluebeard into it. How do I keep the allegory in the forefront? Ideas rumbling in my head with no place to go.

There was this play in my head that I started. It was in a convent, a subtle love scene between Margaret and Monkhouse, in which there was much ado about her idea for depicting gems. She worked in her fairytales, she symbolized it using little finger gestures. He was captivated by your whole idea, not revealing how much till the presentation of shamrock pieces just before the curtain. Not much there yet. Needed time to think it through.

Back to the kitchen. There was hardly enough for Christmas. I decided to make taffy instead of bonbons, it was cheaper. But I did have 3 installments to finish before Christmas, and I had to get those finished somehow. Finally, I had a small following of my food articles, and I could write my essays, if only I could find some time.

I felt desperate one day to do some serious writing. I called around to see if I could do any writing on behalf of Pat Obrien, the young man confused with the convict "Two Gun Crowley," who was being sent up for 20 to 40 years, although everyone seemed to know that he was innocent. I tried to get a magazine to finance an article about my expedition of mercy. Not only could I find no one to finance me, but I couldn't even find anybody to say they would print the finished story. In the end, I got someone to watch Bobby, went to the court of criminal sessions, determined to write the story whether I had a publisher or not. I went first to Father Barry, the Catholic priest interested in the case, because he knows Pat's character to be good. He thought I'd better get right over to the court of criminal sessions before things were finished up so that I could perhaps talk to the mother and the lawyer. He gave me a card to introduce me to either of them. I didn't know how to get there, so I asked him, but he didn't know either, having gone to visit with somebody who knew the way. He advised me to ask the first cop. I met this gentleman on the corner who was rather vague about the directions, and I, being used to Paris, where subways run underground rather than helter-skelter, I made a mistake, and lost a lot of time running up several sets of elevated steps. It was confusing to me, and after asking several other people, I finally found my way to Columbus Circle on the subway. I had to take it to Times Square and then shuttle over to Grand Central. The New York subway system signs were so small on the side that a girl couldn't make them out, and the tracks all seemed to be leading in different directions. Of course, I kept asking and I said to myself, "It was for this that you learn to talk, Suzanne," and then finally I took a train to Grand Central, and another to Canal Street and arrived at the courthouse pretty much out of breath. I was directed to several wrong elevators trying to find the Judge in his court. Then I got on the right elevator, having been told to go to the eighth floor, but the elevator man said Judge Levine was on the fourth floor or vice versa. Just then, I heard someone say, "Hello, Sue." Lo and behold, it was my old friend Eddie Jackson from the *Daily News*. Eddie, a photographer, said, "You get off here with me, and then I'll go up to Judge Levine's with you. I still got that picture I took of you and Johnny coming out of the château." Now, this was very sweet of Eddie to pilot me around and to say that about the Château, because he never did actually take a picture of Johnny and me. In the reporters' room, he found somebody who got me past the guards to judge Levine's court just in time to hear the summation. Anyway, all the people who were closest to the case think he was probably as innocent as you were, including the first judge who sentenced him. There was a lot of monkey business in this trial. He was sentenced to 20-40 years and sent to Sing Sing prison.

Poor Mrs. O'Brien was crying and carrying on about how her son had been framed and that he could get no justice in the court. If she had money, she would be able to get justice for him. I sympathized with her, and she made a meeting time with me for 5 o'clock. But then somebody told her, while my back was turned, that it was the newspaper publicity that sent her son to the penitentiary. So, of course, when I came back, she canceled our appointment. It didn't seem as if a girl could do much good trying to wage a crusade with no arms and no publisher. Eddie Jackson came out to take a picture of the baby. I interviewed the lawyer, and the boy's lawyer told me he had run out of his own money spent pursuing this case. There seemed to be nothing left to prepare an affidavit to present to Governor Roosevelt in the hopes of a pardon.

The newspapers were just filled with articles about the poverty, the dust bowls out west, and growing political struggles in Europe. There were fewer opportunities for fashion articles, but people still ate, and the *New York Herald Tribune* comforted people with food and stories of faraway places related to food. My niche became how to write articles about food that were festive and not expensive, with easily found ingredients. It was not my Great

American novel, but I became known for my tidbits about Europe interlaced with easy, inexpensive recipes or ways to decorate a table. At least I was working! I vowed that when things got better, I would return to Paris.

Through my writings, I could dream of my days in Paris and a time when I could at least write about food, decorations, and holidays as if I were still in Paris, Italy, or Ireland. Most of my articles referenced Paris as if the reader were walking along the Boulevard with me. Outdoor tables with little chairs seemed to symbolize that long, bewitching stretch through the boulevard, calling attention to other elegant and lovely Parisian streets. "Do you remember their fluttering umbrellas beckoning joyously from tree-shaded railway stations at Nanci or Rouen, and Britney watching bright little sailing vessels come in with the tide while leaves tumble down into your cider. In Paris, you actually sit in one place on a platform where branches of a tree reach down, as other diners have croissants with jam. Nothing could possibly speak with more eloquence for a weekend vacation in the country than breakfast every morning in the open air with plenty of light fluffy rolls like the French brioche or croissant with pale yellow pads of fresh country butter, homemade jams and jellies that you would never eat in the city unless you capture their secrets and sparkling glasses with the café au lait." Other articles were "Tricks of the French Chef", Perhaps it sounds more French!

I would not just present the recipe but would inspire memories of times past, people, and environments. Food was more than just throwing food on the table. It was a time for family, for warm memories, for recipes passed down for generations. Food represented our society and life's occasions. I never said that I was French, but certainly my articles gave that impression, and they were all signed Sue Moody (not White). Writing of any kind took me away from my cares of life. I would frequently write,

"Salt your food with humor, season it with wit, sprinkle it all over with a charm of good fellowship, but never poison it with the cares of your life"

I wrote in one article, "when winter sets in and the snowflakes begin to turn into whirling masses, taking on shapes of teddy bears clinging to the branches or the turkey gobbler is winding their way among the mounds of snow, my thoughts begin to dwell upon ideas of Holiday suites; and those yellow cookbooks handed down from my mother and aunts, even from someone else's mother and aunts, have a way of making their presence known in the kitchen with an insistence sort of demand for attention.[9]"

Thanksgiving time was always a great time to get an article published. I noted to my readers that anyone can roast a turkey, but what about everything that goes along with it? That was what made each person's Thanksgiving unique and what made each person's Thanksgiving something to look forward to. And those major holidays suddenly invoked times gone by, centuries of men in top hats and women in silk. An old-fashioned holiday with a setting of turquoise candles and gray nasturtium cloth. A huge bowl of rich reds and yellows, and purples in the center. Dishes that held cucumber pickles, jellies, nuts, and cranberry sauce. Turkey on an oversized platter. And desserts that were like the ones Grandma made, reminding us of old treasures almost forgotten, and the tireless energy that women put into their cooking. Aunt Kate would preserve her strawberries and raspberries from the summer so that in winter, when we were all shivering from the December cold, we could have the sweet taste of summer.

---

[9] Sue Moody, "Old Inn Style: Holiday Treats", original manuscript in the Sue Moody Archives, prepared for the New York Herald Tribune

As if that was not enough, decorate each dessert tart differently.

Summer was the time for casual gatherings and learn from the Swedish to have a Smorgasbord on different levels of the table. Articles of mine told the reader how to plan a party with a buffet so that the host can actually enjoy it as well.

And a birthday is not just about the recipe, but how to make it something special. I quoted a friend, "You cannot rush a cake, you have to add a little relationship into the recipe. The cake should fit the person. The top of the cake would be decorated with flowers, nuts or berries, or swirls of color.[10]" I could bring people back to an easier time when they could bring joy to their family with a simple recipe that didn't require a lot of ingredients. I had gotten good at writing articles about food and joyous occasions amid depression.

Even the football day party gathering could be more than the snacks that accompanied the game. I suggested that the seats be arranged in tiers like a stadium. A tea cart was transformed into one with hot dogs. The host wore a cheerleader costume, and punch was served by a young man dressed as the water boy.

---

[10] Sue moody, "Let Them Eat Cake", New York Herald Tribune, Magazine Section, February 21, 1937

Everything tasted better when served creatively. My articles were made into booklets with all the recipes that I mentioned available from the *NY Herald's Home Institute*. The most successful one was all about Ice Cream.

Just before Halloween, I wrote about a little old woman who lived alone in the hills. As you ride by, you might stop and give her a coin, and then she would tell you everything she knew about the neighbors and what they were up to. Things you would never have dreamed of yourself. She also brilliantly told you things about the moon and what it would do for the crops, predictions of battles and bloodshed on certain hills. She would never dare to cut a tree that grew in a circle planting "the sort of planting is known as a corpse," and "never ride by the light of the slender Moon, you'll be sure to take a tumble." Of course, you listened to their prognostications, hoping just for the good future, the fortune teller gave you. Her spirit was supposed to fly away at a shrill whistle, and she simply flew through the hole in the branches. In twilight evenings, when the children and family were outside, they would often see about actually skimming through this whole in the trees. With stories like that, Halloween should have an Irish flair. Or another Halloween story begins with "autumn leaves, harvest sheaves, and the black and gold crêpe always associated with Halloween has been tangled inward around pirates and pixies for excitingly original decorations that can be relied upon for each party's success. Send out invitations and watch your children come running, yelling that 'Halloween's in the air'".[11]

In another article, I referenced Alsace, "there's a great deal to be said for the blending of races. Like the blending of sauce. It sometimes brought out the best in each ingredient that went into the pot. My auspicious arrival in Strasburg made us think that the Franco-German blend. We arrived in Strasbourg one evening at dusk after a 44 km jog through the Vosges mountains on a bicycle. Whenever we asked passersby in French on the Quai Saint Nicholas or the hotel Beau Rivage, they invariably turned out to be German-speaking. When we asked the question, and what we considered fair German, they were always French-speaking. So, by the time we had located the Beau Rivage, we were nearly starved and so fatigued. The whole idea of two languages in one town was exhausting, to state it mildly. But after finding the Beau Rivage and tasting at first Alsatian cooking, we were enthused enough to cancel a week's trip to Munich, and we instead spent our entire vacation right there at the Beau Rivage." After my story, I then gave a couple of Alsatian recipes.[12]

---

[11] Sue moody, "Halloween Hilarity", New York Herald Tribune, Magazine Section, October 25, 1936
[12] Sue Moody, "Well Blended", New York Herald Tribune, This Week, Magazine Section, June 1936

Now I was back in Paris to a nightmare worse than the Depression of seven years earlier.

The *International Herald*, which had hired me to go to Paris now to write about food and fashion, had reserved us an apartment in a southwest suburb of Paris, in Meudon. How could I possibly say no! I had been to Meudon in 1929. It was famous as a town for "cures," famous for its hills and good air. It was a renowned county seat with goats roaming the hills and picturesque farms that had lasted for centuries. Madame de Pompadour had a large chateau in the neighborhood. She liked to be there and play at being a country girl. It was a place where children played on the streets and women socialized. I had an apartment in the highest house in the town with a magnificent view of Paris. But now all I saw was sorrow and despair. Paris had emptied, but Meudon … all everyone talked about was leaving if they had not left before the Germans marched in.

Chapter 5
Topaz

You can't win a war without supplies. My friends in America kept saying, before I left for Paris. How bad could it be in Paris, they asked? I am sure that you can always make an omelet, maybe Poullard style. They had no idea. An omelette! We were happy if we had one potato. But after decades of struggling to be taken seriously, I was finally in Paris as a journalist. I didn't think long or hard about the potential dangers. I was expected to be writing articles about food and fashion. I now had a position with UPI and the *Herald Tribune* to go to Paris and report on the food and the fashion. That was the best that I could hope for as a female Journalist. Rarely did women get political assignments. But I would be in Paris, and my years of studying French and visiting there several times before would surely help me to make the most of this career move. My husband, Johnny, was at first not happy about the position and my leaving, but for me, it was the opportunity of a lifetime. Suddenly, Johnny changed his attitude and pushed me to go. He said that he would send me money to help. I thought that he was being good to me, encouraging me to go. Johnny had always said that he would be supportive of my career, even if he had never been before. He knew from the beginning, when we first met, that I was not like the other sorority girls and that I wanted a career.

Johnny White was an older boy whose real name was Llewelyn White. He came up to me one day at a party. We exchanged niceties, and then we occasionally passed notes in the hallway near the Journalism department, but we never had much of a conversation. I just kind of brushed him off because Johnny sometimes walked away mid-conversation. Sometimes, I thought that he was so rude! I later found out that he had a bet with someone that he could get 6 kisses from me! He put me in the position of a marionette, with him pulling the strings. I was furious because it seemed like a performance that we were going through. I wanted to be in control as I was with Chicita or Madgie, the horses that I had trained and ridden over the years.

The day before school ended, my Junior year of college, before my summer at the ranch, Johnny said something loving to me. I had to laugh him off in case it was a joke. I didn't want to be a sentimental fool. But then I was worried because maybe he didn't think that I cared about him. I wasn't sure that I did. Boys were such a waste of my time. Then Johnny asked me if I was afraid of him. I told him that I would never be afraid of a man as long as I believed in myself. I went into a long tirade about what I wanted for my life. "I'm afraid that I don't know if I can make a success of

being a writer, but I need to try. I needed to commit myself to it."
I went on to say that I had "some very old-fashioned ideas about
marriage, and that once married, you have to commit yourself to
that. I cannot reconcile marriage with the way I want to live my
life. I told him that I believed in his sincerity, that he cares for me,
but you need to believe in mine.[13] I wanted to find my way and
not be responsible to anyone." When I told Johnny what my
thoughts were, he said that he was glad for the sake of our nation
that there weren't too many women like me! Perhaps Johnny was
afraid of me. He wrote to me a few times over the summer while I
was at the ranch. I wrote him back cordially.

When I returned in the Fall of my senior year, we had our first
date. I must admit that Johnny treated me as I liked to be treated,
as a person with intelligence and understanding. I had told many
a man that I would never marry. If responsibility came up, I
simply wanted to turn and run. I just wanted to write. I wanted to
just stay in Colorado or Wyoming, but I had to come back to help
my mother. I am not a woman to be put in a high-backed chair and
adored. I wrote to Johnny when we were first getting to know each
other, " I believe that you are making me into your dream girl.
And I don't fit."[14]

---

[13] September 4, 1923
[14] September 12, 1923

Over and over, I told Johnny not to treat me as a girlfriend, just as a friend. But Johnny sent roses, and well, the roses did make the whole day sweet. And he wrote, "There's one rose that fades not in Picardy/ It's the rose that I wear in my heart."[15] Whenever I see pink roses, I think of Johnny, who sent them to me for my birthday and for no reason at all. I remember that he told me to be happy – just be happy. For the little pink rose in my heart will smile.

Johnny's brother asked if anyone else was doing anything at that school. All I ever heard about was Sue Moody. I hoped to never lose him as a friend and would sooner never see him again than lose him as a friend. I wrote to Johnny that he would soon forget me, but until that time, when he became a successful writer, I would make desperate grabs to keep myself seated on his comet's tail."[16]

Betty and I talked about going with Johnny to Europe. We planned how we would all go as friends, telling everyone that we were cousins. I planned this scheme that we would take on names like Genevieve and Pauletta. I thought that I would get there by being a horse trainer. I loved the horses and was so good with them. The trainer at the ranch was going to teach me more. I could

---

[15] Sept 28, 1933 references lyrics from a song.
[16] July 31 1923

buy some green horses in the winter, train them, and then sell them for a profit. Dreams of horses and writing, and independence seemed to fade when Johnny suddenly declared his love for me. No, just be my friend, I declared, but all the love letters came flooding in from Johnny. I was swept away by his sweet words and the fairy tale of my being his princess and his being my knight in shining armor. How does a young girl fight the two strands of her being? It was the late 1920s, it was supposedly roaring, and women had the right to vote, and perhaps we could now have it all. Silly girl. Well, I was young.

Oh, the love letters that we wrote to each other. I was hooked. I told him how I dreamed of him, and without him, I was as lost as if I were Alice in Wonderland. "I am in Wonderland. That is, when I am with you. In my mind, I am always with you." I actually wrote, "I love you until I have the chokiest, smothered feeling." We were both writers and knew just what to say for this fairytale. Reading his letters was like little girls getting candy. I often wrote him poems when we were far from each other, such as:

Lightning
There is a solitude in seeing you
Followed by your company when you are gone
You are like Heaven's veins of Lightning.
I cannot see until afterward

How beautiful you are.

There is a blindness in seeing you.

Followed by the sight of you when you are gone.

I never wanted to lose Johnny as a friend or a confidant, but he was becoming more of a lover. We would take walks, take out horses, and sit together writing when we were together. It was my fairytale come true, and I was mesmerized by him; I loved being intimate with him. We would lie together and make our plans for the future. I really believed that I might have it all, that he respected my desire to work and write. My only other task was to keep Margaret Wallace away from Johnny. She was infatuated with him, even though I helped her pledge and get into the sorority. She kept reminding me that I said that Johnny and I were only friends!

I was in love, but with that affection came a flood of insecurities. I worried about not being good enough, about losing him. Sometimes, I was afraid to write because I might say something wrong. Other times, I wrote because I didn't want Johnny to forget me. How often I felt unworthy of him. I wrote, "I do not feel now that I am what you'd visualized in your picture of the lady you could adore as your queen." Sometimes I thought that I had a dual personality, and I wanted one to succumb to the other.

I could be hypnotized and have one of me submerged in the other, and pray that the best one wins.

Johnny quoted an article by DW Griffith to me in which he wrote that no matter how beautiful a woman was of face and form, if she lacked one important element — personality — she couldn't hold her own with women who had it. And I just glowed because he said, "My Sudy girl" (that was one of his nicknames for me) "had it all, absolutely all the attributes of the loveliest woman plus a little bit of an angel."

He vowed to always get me "Picardy roses." He wrote to me from the song, "that the rose that lasts is the one you keep in your heart." He then added, "I will have to always buy you a pink Picardy rose every year to renew the one in your heart. No matter how poor we are or what happens, I will sell my watch or anything to get you that rose." He told me that, "You will be the prettiest and funniest at the party, so that you will hear people jealously say that's Johnny White's girl." I always thought that I didn't want to get married, but Johnny was so good to me. It was the fairy tale fantasy that held onto the tail of the comet now. My response was that, "You are so wonderful that I get positively shaky for fear I might disappoint you or disillusion you, or not take care of you as you deserve. It's an awfully responsible piece of work God's given to me." There goes my lack of confidence again.

Our relationship was the news around campus. Suddenly, everyone was involved in Johnny and my relationship, pushing it to go further. People told me that if I loved him that I should wear his pin and show the world that we were together, especially to Margaret Wallace. But what if it didn't work out? And then they all just keep asking, "When will you be married?"

By Thanksgiving, Johnny and I had declared our love, but we were so far away from each other. I was in Lawrence, Kansas, and he had graduated and had a job at a newspaper in Kansas City, 28 miles away. But without a car and having to depend on the bus, it was so very far away. And he had to work, and I had school. It had been only five months since our first letters. All that time away from each other, while I was in college, he was true to me. I would share my deepest thoughts and most profound fears with him. I told him, "I have hopeless hopes and unrealized dreams. Will it be all up to me, and if I ever fail us, it would be awful. "When all the world has been going wrong, there has always been a wonderful realization to keep me going. The realization of you."

Every time a special delivery came, I got so excited. I would just dream, reminisce, and picture that first time that Johnny took me in his arms and kissed me so gently, and put me to bed. I didn't know how I got along before him. He was my everything now, so I truly believed. He wrote to me, "Oh my darlin', you are mine!

And just this morning, you sat on the train with me and held me close, and patted my hand. Every pat said that you are my nice little Sudy girl." I replied, "I will be such an awfully unusual person by the time I am 40 because every time you look at me as you do, and every time you hug me tight, and every time you even pat my hand, I feel like such an angel!"

Van Dyke wrote a poem that resonated with me, and I sent Johnny a copy.

Who seeks for heaven alone to save his soul
May keep the path, but will not reach the goal,
While he who walks in love may wander far,
But God will bring him where the blessed are"

I really respected Van Dyck, but could I do what he said and wait five years to get married and have my career going first, or would I lose Johnny then?

I wrote to Johnny,

"I felt like a slim crescent moon in a green sky. When I walked past the building, it loomed nearby. And when I looked up in the vast sky alone, it was so tiny. That's the way I am. I seem to be something when you are here. But when you are not, and I'm alone—I'm only a very small lady." How did I become so dependent on a man? Is that what love is supposed to be? Giving up yourself for someone else?

We shared our feelings about family and our early life. He was supposed to be, according to society and his mother, a rough and tumble boy, but rather, he loved to sit by a stream and write. I told him how my mother always wanted me to be a sweet little girl in frilly dresses. I doubted that my mother ever forgave me for not being the daughter she wanted. Johnny also loved books and acting, and singing. He was not the son that his mother wanted, either. As far back as he could remember, Johnny said that he felt like he was a stranger in his own home. Johnny wrote to me, "I learned to take my little boy's dreams and hopes, and plans only to my father. That used to make her furious at him, and at me." Johnny went on and mentioned how the Chinese gave little girls they did not want to their gods by throwing them into the Yangtze River. He told me, "I felt like she would do that to me if she could. So, I just closed my heart to her. It was bad enough when Dad was preaching, and he went travelling, that I endured a hell on earth. There were years when I scorned my Mother and despised my brother. Periodically, I ran away from home. When Dad would come home, he would take me to the side and try to get me to understand. Poor, poor Dad! Once, when my brother and I were scuffling, I accidentally hit him in the stomach, and when she came in and saw him writhing on the floor, she called me a little beast. And when Dad came home, she told him that I had tried to kill my brother and that it was the trash blood of the Whites that made me that way. And so, we grew farther apart, and it became 2 against 2. Once I enlisted in the army and a train whisked me away to camp, and uncertain death, her remorse set in. She came to the training camp once and fed my buddies and acted in a way she never had before. *Loving*. She even told me that she might accept the military but said she had bigger plans for me."

As we each unveiled our souls and deepest thoughts, our families, and our hopes and dreams, Johnny and I became closer and wrote to each other almost every day. It was like a fantasy story where two lost souls had found each other and would go off on their own, and truly believed that they would live happily ever after.

I wrote to Johnny, "I was thinking that it would be fun to go off for a year under a nom de plume and not write to anyone or hear from anyone. Just live – with no accounting whatever to anyone. Maybe we would like it so well that we'd never completely give up that freedom."

I didn't want to end up like my family. They were solid, moral, self-satisfied, good Quakers. Not the least demonstrative, and just to damn conservative about their affections." Then I told him, "Someday, we will be collaborating and hearing the world talk of the grand stuff we'll turn out."

On Valentine's Day, my mother always said that I should send a thank you for all the flowers, but I always said that I didn't want the flowers boys sent me; they could be dandelions if they came with real passion. "What do I care for those bunches of hay?" And I would rather have a poetic verse Johnny wrote instead. I read Edna St Vincent Millay, and all I wanted to do was to write a volume of love poems. It would be the richest of all love verses. Like rich wine and cyclamen, like the flower which was so fragrant it seemed stained with heart's blood to Johnny. It should be published in a deep purple volume with cyclamen lettering.

I wanted to be like the orchids that I love best. We must take care of our orchids, knowing that we had them and that they require tender treatment. If we should lose our sensitiveness, or our ability to feel deeply, we would also lose our appreciation for beautiful things and all of our ability to write. And we'd regenerate into very common, ordinary people."

I grew up believing that my knight in shining armor would appear on a white horse and rescue me. Was Johnny my Knight and I, his Princess? I began to talk to Johnny about my fairy tales and beliefs in former lives. I told him that I believed that I must have lived another life with knights and princesses, my life had always been tied to horses and all they suggested, and even the politics I'd been involved in were related to my former life.

Gradually, I told him about my past life as a princess. There was a lot of intrigue in the Royal court that I was in. I even know a man today who was the Prime Minister back then. One night, I sat on my front porch, and my scarf blew over to another man, and we looked at each other strangely, and I said, "We knew each other before and planned a campaign together like tonight?" And he said, "Yes, Princess." I said, "Who were you then?" And he calmly said, "I was your Prime Minister." Johnny and I developed pet names for each other as he went along with my stories. I called him my Gentio, and he called me his princess Sudy.

We sent each other poems. I sent him a William Rose Benet's verse,

"Scurvy doctrine that love's tambourine

A love that is fond and true

Is exactly like a tamed dragon

I'm telling this to you!

A perfectly tangible dragon
With perfectly tangible paw.
You could climb a mountain in Argentina,
But you'd know it was."

I explained to Johnny that there were dragons in every kingdom, dragons of all kinds. "The dragon came and went last night," I told him of my fears. "The dragon is dangerous, and I fear the dragon. It appears and reappears. I've decided that the only thing that I can do is to do my work, work hard, and ignore the dragons of my life. Someday, maybe I can slay the dragon and be free of it. I fear that I am not strong enough to slay the dragon by myself." I went on,

"You are my knight, and you must fight for me. You are my strong knight. The knight has to be there for all the little girls who need them, my knight. But you do not even know half of the danger. I have never told you, because I do not like to talk to you about unhappy things. If ever such a dragon as this one could be slain, I know that you could do it — but it's such a monstrous one. And the Prime Minister would rather it were left alive. So, how could you ever hope to gain his approval? Cause I want it killed. Did we ever think that we would have to leave the court and defy the Prime Minister? But if you could rid the court of the dragon, then the whole court would be so proud of you." I was now reduced to that little girl cowering behind my knight in shining armor.

I wove the story, my fairy tale. "Today, I am sending a token to the bravest knight, a seal bearing your likeness in armor. I drew it myself. I always know that you are afraid of nothing. I know just as I knew that one night you would give me diamonds and pearls, that you will always take care of me because I am now forever your princess. Being your princess, I need your strong arms around me. You have used your strength to save me hundreds of times. And now I quite depend on you and seem to be unable to face dragons without you.

Gentio, did you kill the only big old dragon that I was ever afraid of? And you were so brave about it. Oh, Gentio, so now, I should not be afraid of anything, now that I have you!"

I remembered this song:
"In a kingdom of our own
With little Cupid on the throne
Prince and Princess we will be
And we'll be as happy as a king should be. Every afternoon at 3
We will sip our royal tea
You'll be the K I N G then

I'll be the Queen
In a kingdom of our own
And H A P P Y we'll be
In a kingdom of our own."

"I'd been so quiet and good. I never imagined that I could change so much. All I want now is to love you and make you happy. Just to look into your Gentian eyes. Just care for me, Gentio. I love you so." I rambled on to him. "Remember my brave knight, bravest of all, whenever any dragon would fight you, my ring will protect you from all hardships because it is a gift of the faeries, to me, for you. Only if you did not believe and were perfectly sure, then you need never be afraid. As long as you have the ring, it would hurt the faeries, and they would cause you to be wounded deeply by the ring. So, from the minute that you put it on, you must believe what I tell you, you need never be afraid as long as you wear it."

Oh, our letters were so filled with fantasies, dreams, and fairy tales. Johnny wrote:

"We are Pierrot and Pieret, and will travel to Japan and Switzerland, and then have our children named Bobby and Betty. Everything will be so much fun." The only problem was that

Pierot and Pierret, written in 1924, were brother and sister. Were we brother, sister, best friends, lovers, or all of them?

And then his new nickname for me was Celia. I was Princess Celia, and Johnny wrote:

"Celia's joy could not be told
Except by her eloquent eyes
And Celia's voice could not be heard
Except in soft little cries."

He wrote to me, "Precious! I love you too everlastingly much to lead you into a path where the naughty thorns might reach out and hurt your precious little feet. I would put my life between the woman I worship and danger--- danger of any sort.

And those babies of ours--- when I come breathlessly into the room and fall on my knee beside the bed, when I see there my angel wife hallowed by the most magnificent sacrifice it is in Her power to make, when I peer down through swimming eyes at the tiny bit of life curled in the crook of her arm, my son, my daughter, my flesh and blood." The thorns and dragons were starting to be revealed. As we began to talk about marriage, Johnny revealed his dire indebtedness. So, we postponed the wedding until he could pay off his debts.

Back to the real world. I began looking for a job as I prepared to graduate from college with a degree in English. I contacted the mayor of Kansas City, who was a family friend. He said that it would be easier for me to get a job if I weren't married. It might be hard the first month financially, but then I would get a job. We put the wedding off again until we had jobs.

I then went to Denver for a job in advertising, a place with 2 stores for women's clothing. The agency did all sorts of wonderful campaigns, many related to Paris and all things French. I loved the chance to be creative and hoped I would get that job. I had the best time going around, talking to people, looking for a job, and sharing my ideas. I was always good with clothing when I had no money. I loved hats, so I took an old black hat, wet it, re-blocked it, and after it dried, I added dried flowers to it. I loved scarves. They're so jaunty and careless, I was going to have a purple one next. Maybe I could paint one. I presented my idea of a shopping column in the papers for the Denver Dry Goods store. It would be an out-of-town shopper's column. I would look at what was coming in before it arrived and create a chatty column. I would camp out in the receiving room and make friends with someone from each department. I immediately got the job doing advertising. My boss asked me to come up with a campaign, "What would a Denver girl wear if she were to meet the Prince of

Wales?" It was to be a full-page ad featuring a full-length portrait of the Prince and copy on both sides. All the lessons from my sister and sorority sisters now played into my marketing and journalism. Maybe my two halves were coming together, and maybe I could marry Johnny and have babies with him. More exciting than a wedding was when copies of my Prince of Wales ad came out and gave me credit in Women's Wear Daily, a national paper.

My job would start part-time, but when a position in advertising actually opened up, it would be full-time. People came to see me at the store. I really enjoyed it and looked forward to making a career there until I was told by the Vice President that it would never become a full-time position. Women were not hired for marketing; they didn't know what people wanted. I was flabbergasted, after all, it was for women's clothing. I was distraught after so many successes, and I reached out to Johnny for ideas. I only stayed in Denver for four months until I resigned (July to November 1924). They wrote a glowing letter about the work that I had done, and I would hold onto that letter. I soon received an offer from a newspaper in San Francisco, so Johnny and I would be even further separated.

Meanwhile, Johnny was writing political editorials for the Kansas City paper. He often wrote of struggling for content, things that he could write about, and not anger the Senator. Johnny wrote a piece about the Teapot Dome scandal and the bribes that went to the highest level of government concerning oil leases. In another, he was giving heck to the senate for overstepping the chief executive's powers when they voted 47 to 34 to oust Secretary Denby.

We discussed and he wrote about LaFolette's nomination and how Smith's percentage was climbing. I felt like I was helping him with his more serious articles.

I wondered how we would manage being so far away from each other, so I wrote to Johnny, "I decided that I will get my Master's degree as soon as I can. I just think that being a Professor is quite wonderful and that while some people belong in business, others need to write and teach and create. I could teach High School, but with a Master's, I could follow you wherever you are and be a Professor. I could teach English or advertising. I can't go on with doing advertising if I am not in a big city and not respected or considered qualified because I am a woman."

In 1924, Johnny wrote for the *New Republic* (a progressive journal) and some articles briefly for the *San Francisco Telegraph*. It was short-lived, our being together, but I hoped that we could find a way and get married. We had to find a way to work in the same city. Meanwhile, the other issue was that Johnny's mother adamantly objected to our marriage, claiming that I didn't know how to make a proper home. My parents objected because he didn't have any money saved and didn't have a secure job yet. Only the brothers and sisters saw how much we loved each other. But Johnny told me that his main venture in life was to make me happy. He wrote that to me; happiness meant that behind every short story that he sold, he would lay a fur coat, and silky underthings, a hat, a car, a fine horse, a trip. "Whatever I can lay at your feet." But then I thought about Johnny's mother. She was always condemning me. Is it that I am not pretty enough or that I am too ambitious for a girl? She did say that my face had character. I guess that is a good thing. When I was 7 or 8 years old, I suddenly realized that I was not good-looking. So, being resourceful, I decided that I have to have a wonderful personality. I might be able to get by on that alone and make people forget my looks. But then I thought that if I am to make it in this world, good looks count for more than anything. So, I started to diet, and the worst thing was sleeping all night on rags so that I could have wavy locks! My life ambition was now resolved into a two-part proposition:

1- To be able to wear an evening dress divinely, and at the same time

2- To be able to ride a cow-pony as gracefully as a beautiful dancer can follow every slightest movement of her partners.

These goals mean that it was not just about good looks but also poise and charm, and all that went with a lovely part of lovely people. But it also meant that I would not be soft but still be an outdoor girl, receptive to the wonders of nature and the hidden trails that life presents. The second part was easier for me than the first. Looking back, where was the goal of being a successful writer? Had it all been subsumed by the fairy tale, which was already showing cracks?

The wedding plans changed again, and finally Johnny's mother wrote a letter, "I am becoming so excited over your approaching marriage, darling boy. I know your blessed children will make each other very happy. She sent a list of things she would offer us, like some plated table silver, the quilt that Grandma White gave her, a pair of red cross blankets of Daddy's." She asked to please keep in touch and that although they doubted that they could afford to come to the ceremony, "our two hearts are with you both from this moment forward." I decided that we all had to come together and offered to Johnny that we should let his father marry us. It seemed that everyone was rising to the occasion. I would as well.

I gradually changed my ambitions and decided that I could not write as well as Johnny.

I suddenly declared that my job would be to keep Johnny in condition, and true to his purpose (not like Hawthorne's wife – all locked up in a garret until you'd have to produce or starve). "I would keep you fresh so that you might never get stale on ideas. That way, I could reconcile my conscience, and I could make your triumphs my own.

If you sell your stories, I am not going to work after we first get married, I'll just spend more time learning how to manage a house. I don't know a thing about it, and after I'd learn and vacation awhile, I'd be in so much better shape to manage a job and our home, too. Oh, we will be happy forever and forever." Another fairy tale of happily ever after. (The fairy tale that I was told did not include being a working woman!)

I dreamed about my fairy tale, but still wrote when I could. I now wrote about being a bride.

I wrote stories about different brides, and actually got these stories published in various small-press journals. I was proud of them, and they read as follows:

"There is no more blissful kiss than that of being a bride. All the world knows that, and probably no one wishes more than that bride herself to cherish that lore she senses that being a bride to some young man just starting is not altogether Stardust and Roses." Scarcely, two weeks passed before the archvillain, "the family budget," walked into the circle. That was when the bride's ingenuity would need to serve her well if she cared for the bridal lore. It was time to stretch the pennies to the limit. I decided to interview 3 brides.

First bride. How do you make money last and make their personal surroundings as charming as when they were bachelor girls? Dorothy turned indignantly to me. Just come with me, please, and she led me to her bedroom. They sat at the most adorable dressing table imaginable. It was flowered Cretonne skirt (lightly woven cotton) standing out primarily from its emerald gray top, a gray framed mirror hanging above by a blue cord. On the glossy top of the table were repose bottles and jars painted the same blue as the cord with large pastel roses to match those in the cretonne of the skirt. It looked like a corner of the garden and seemed to inspire Dorothy's dainty loveliness. But the surprise was that she had made it all herself. This was the way she explained it: "First, I had the top put on two brackets in the wall, just a piece of white wood like a pantry shelf, and fastened on in the same way. I painted it gray with a quick-drying enamel paint that can be washed. I made the skirt from cretonne and fastened it on the pleats as you see with strong upholstery tacks. I painted the frame of a long, old mirror gray and hung it by that blue cord I had bought at a picture framing shop. The jars from my cold cream and powder were in the bottles for witch hazel astringent or toilet water, which I painted with a color prepared for treating glass." She pointed to a lovely, grand marble box where she had glued a reproduction of an 1830s painting. That box held everything else: my cotton, cold cream, and my manicure things. The skirt of her table was pulled aside down the middle of the front a little gray enamel pail was revealed. "That's where I throw my cotton when I'm done. I only have to empty it once a week. Dorothy's table might well have had shelves put in halfway to accommodate even more things. But this simple table made for a beautiful boudoir."

Second bride: If I had been surprised at Dorothy's ingenuity, I was no less amazed at Betty's.

The second bride had just completed her dressing table and insisted upon giving me implicit instructions. She said, "I made it from two flat boards and some old packing boxes my mother-in-law had in her basement. I cut the boxes apart and put them together again, so they form two upright, three-shelf cabinets. On top of these upright cabinets, which I placed apart just the way they want to be, like parentheses, I nailed the two boards. Yes, they made the top. Then I sandpapered all the rough edges and painted it with enamel paint with a soft lavender color. You see how I lowered the top of my table to put Jute over the edge of the upright cabinets for 2 inches all the way around. That was very useful because when the time came to string wire around for hanging my curtains, I had the means to hide this wire. I used plain green glaze chintz for my curtains, cutting it in half, vertically, to form the center opening and to make the material easier to handle. I made the edges with bias binding, just a little darker shade of green. Last of all, I bought a piece of glass just the size of my tabletop and placed it over the top. It is ideal because it is so easily cleaned. Then with my green crystal candle, my lavender pail, candles, and darker green of my bias binding, I found I had made this corner of the room one of the most alluring in the apartment."

Third bride: I suggested that since Betty had such a modern Parisian air about her table with its plain green chintz to match the window drapes, she might also hang her walls with Picasso prints. She laughed, saying, "They were a bit dear, and then we went to call on Jean as if an answer to a talk of Paris. Jean, who was only a few weeks married, let us into her little boudoir trousseau, which was a wedding gift from her mother. It just looks so adorably Paris, but I had to make some accessories to go with it." She said that she put powder in cold cream jars, toilet, and perfume in flasks, all from the least expensive shop in the neighborhood. "I painted them with glossy black paint. Then the bottles were painted over in white with the words powder, cleansing cream, astringent, toilet water, all in French.' On the last bottle, she explained that it held her husband's shaving lotion." Surely, all three dressing tables were bride-like. And very special.

Now I would be a bride, and worry about the finances, making beautiful things, cooking great dinners, all to make my man happy, because I thought that Johnny was now my knight in shining armor. Why do little girls grow up believing in fairies and being a princess? They believe that a fearless, handsome knight will come and sweep them off their feet. He will be strong and brave and be able to fight off all the fierce dragons that might attack us in our lives. The stories the fairytales read to us each night permeate our dreams, and even if we know that they are not real, we want to believe in a version of that. So, when Johnny came and told me that he would take care of me forever, hold me tight, and make me feel beautiful, I believed him. And he was also caught up in the fairytale. He was my knight, he called me his princess, and perhaps because we lived so far away from each other most of the time, and only saw each other occasionally, letters could keep the fairytale alive. We continued to write long letters of love and poetry almost every day. There were long letters about how great our future, plans of running off to New York, and me as his wife, taking care of him. Rarely did reality come into play in those first few years.

Little girls are told stories about Cinderella, Snow White, and how Prince Charming swoops her up. Now that I had my Prince Charming, I dreamed of a beautiful wedding, being a bride, and going on a great honeymoon. Surely, there was a story in there.

Honeymoon, scene one: The big train station. Noise and bustle. Then, through the great doors, comes a little princess. She hesitates for a moment on the threshold, looking. A wild rush. Dropping off her bags. Kisses and smothered little cries while her trunk is checked by Robyn. Celia was waiting for a taxi for 20 minutes when they arrived at the Riviera, a magnificent hotel overlooking the bay outdoor the Presidio. Mr. White's room? Yes, sir, boy! I'll wait down in the lobby, says Robyn. Do you have everything in your bag? Good, the trunk will not be here until later, probably. Breathlessly, Celia opens her bags and dresses for her day, their day. Her little heart is running away with itself tonight. She thought, I will go to sleep in his arms. Oh, dear God, I am so happy. The elevator door opens, and he steps out. He sweeps a look at her from head to foot, an unbelievable picture. Can this be my sweetheart, radiant, lovely, divine? Celia comes swiftly to him with wild blushes, making her face 10 times more beautiful. He takes her moist hands in his, and then, unable to restrain himself, kisses her right there in the lobby. Amused, she glances back and forth. Newlyweds but not quite. 'Quick, sweetest,' he said, 'we must hurry. We are due there in half an hour.' In the taxi, Gentile, can we afford all this? 'Never you worry about that precious. There's more to come, but we've only rented that bridal suite for this night. Tomorrow, we start South. We're going by boat to Pasadena. Wasn't the old man nice to give me two weeks off from work? Tomorrow, we will drive through open country and see miles and miles of grapes, white ribbons of road stretching away in the distance. California in winter is so beautiful.' We drove up to a little white stucco house with roses, thousands of bushes that promise full bloom in the spring. One can always close his eyes and see the blossoms now. This is where the minister lives. You will adore them both. The retired Jendiya asked if we had everything. Let's see a wedding ring, the license, all as it should be. Here we are as our cab waits, it's rented by the hour. Bless you, Mrs. Whitaker, for keeping the roses. Mrs. Whitaker has kept them fresh and waters them ever since morning. I don't remember what else was said, but suddenly all I heard was "I now pronounce you man and wife." We had a lovely wedding dinner for two in the wedding suite. Thank God this moment has been sanctioned by God and lovers. It will live forever in my memory that one moment, when my Robin drank in the marvel of his sweetheart's precious body. The adventure begins with two weeks of unalloyed pleasure. Sheer happiness, and then back to the heavenly little apartment within a stone's throw of the Bay. Hours and days of wonderment and surprise as the ventures begin in earnest for Celia and Robin."

That was my dream of our wedding, how I had envisioned it. But the reality was that we had no money for a honeymoon suite or a taxi. It was just another fantasy, a fairy tale, a dream, and not our reality. But in a story, I can be anyone and go anywhere.

Johnny responded: "And then I would go carefully over every pearl of mem'ry string --- like a devout worshipper — lest I should miss one single pearl. I would live again the moments when your love has worked its miracles."[17] He continued, " With you, I know that I can do anything in the world. Because it will not be a case of you and I – but US! Without you, I would just be a non-entity. Always dreaming – ever despairing of seeing my dreams come true."

---

[17] Johnny wrote "The Ozone Taster" April 1925 while at Kansas City Post
Harry S White, father of Johnny was financial secretary at Oklahoma City University in July 1925

But now, I was away from him again, in Paris with our son and dog. I had believed in fairy tales. A knight on a shiny white horse with a jeweled harness and bells would come and scoop me up, and we would live happily ever after. He would slay all the dragons that terrified me and shower me with necklaces and gems. He would take care of me forever.

What happened to the fairy tale? Is it just a story that men tell little girls to keep them in their place? No letters from Johnny now, no money, no fairytales.

Chapter 6
Pearls

In July 1925 Johnny got a position at the University of South Dakota in Vermillon SD. We would finally be able to live together. It was only $2500 a year, $300 a month during the school year. He tried to get me excited by saying that it is not that far from Wyoming and the ranch that I had loved. I wrote to Johnny, "--- when all the wildness and haunting stillness of the Wyoming mountains shelters the Sacred Love I shall give to you, and when you at last sleep--- with your wife ever so tightly crushed against the big, big heart of you __"

We would get married at the courthouse and then make our way there." Perhaps I could get a school teaching job since I don't have my Masters degree yet. A real honeymoon would have to wait, but it would be an adventure later when we could afford it.

In June Johnny went ahead and found a wonderful place for us and rented it. It was a bungalow that was available for rent in the Fall. It belonged to a deaf-mute woman, so that was probably why it wasn't well advertised. It was built by Miss Eldridge who was a teacher of Spanish and the wife of the Dean of the University. It was surrounded by trees, on the edge of town. It had a big screened-in porch, a large and wonderfully rich garden, and a double garage. Downstairs were two front rooms, which I imagine were for dining, a kitchen, and a bedroom. Upstairs there were two rooms and a bath. Both upstairs rooms could probably be rented to students. The garage might also be rented. It rented for $50 but the rooms could be rented for 15-25 a room. The demand for student rooms was great and I would enjoy that. It was modern and had light fixtures, a bath, soft water, screens, and storm windows.

Adventures were always so much better in our dreams than in reality. Johnny and I wanted an adventure, an adventure together. We had worked in Lawrence, Kansas, Kansas City, Denver Colorado, and San Francisco but we were rarely in the same city together. We wanted to get married but could barely afford to even see each other by living in two separate households. Now that Johnny got a job as a Professor of Journalism at the University of South Dakota we headed out there. We had decided that this would be a great adventure. I hardly knew what to expect. The reality of it all can not be explained in real terms. I dug through a box that I had taken to Paris, thinking that I would find a publisher for short stories, and found the little story.

I so despised living there. Trapped in a little house, alone amongst the frozen tundra I wrote a story about what my life felt like in that desolation called South Dakota.

I had always dreamed of adventures and made up stories that my parents were fearless, a swashbuckler hunting with Roosevelt in the darkest Africa because he was bored, and that my father cruised the seven seas in search of adventure. But the reality was that my father had some apartments in Lawrence and had just died at home of heart failure in a café. The circumstances surrounding that tragedy comprise a deep mystery that I could only pack with my imagination. But when I had ridden my horses in Wyoming I always thought of going back out west and having more of an adventure so when Johnny got his position in Vermillion South Dakota we thought that now we could have a real adventure going there. Our friends in Kansas City tried to dissuade us and we only scoffed at their fears. I told them that they were Jayhawkers waxing fat and lazy. Friends continued to try to dissuade us, warning us of the perils of our proposed adventure. We should have listened to them! So I turned it into this little story.

We knew not much of these Dakotas, only from the maps that I had procured. I also read about the Scandinavians and Germans that had come to populate it along with the Sioux Indians. With maps of the great Nova Scandinavia, as they called it (very few maps were available and there was little information), we learned that there were two Dakotas, North, and South, and that the land was close to the territories of Iowa and Minnesota. In Nebraska, there seemed to be very little information, which was distressing because we would have to press across the whole state to reach our goal. We secured lumber enough to construct a stout boat with which we proposed, after fitting it with a means of locomotion, to push it up the Missouri River as far as we might. I had in the meantime quite luckily, as chance would have it, encountered a young man who claimed to have been in the Dakotas. He offered his proof of a frozen ear, part of which had fallen off. This son of a hearty north person told me frankly that at an early point, we might encounter ice flows in Missouri and be obliged to take to the open country with dogs and sled.

On a Saturday in late August, we set sail to use the expression common to explorers. Although as a matter of fact, the little craft propelled itself and us with no more than the combustible gas engine we'd provisioned for the expedition, along with quantities of salted pork, beans, salt biscuit, corn beef as well as fruits of all sorts. We also provided ourselves with ample protection against the elements in the way of clothing, bedding, and personal belongings. Aside from what we wore, we had our tent and Johnny had his trusty gun. Our new friend from the Dakotas had agreed to accompany us partway but had no desire to return to his former home. He was to act as a guide and in truth he appeared to bear the marks of his craft. We were scarcely outside of Kansas City when he began to tell us venturesome tales of the country to which we were going. We listened to his accounts of battles in which he single-handedly rescued himself from animals and Indians. He noted that the Sioux Indians were a brave yet nonetheless generous race and our informant dwell among them as he extolled their virtues. As he began his fascinating narrative we peppered him with questions, some of which he answered and some he only shrugged his shoulders. Then, on the evening of the third day as we climbed Council Bluffs he began to warn us of the city called Sioux City. Tribes of other Indians he said had come in to pollute the pure Sioux stock here. They had introduced fire water and electric lights, driving the real Sioux away. They made it into a commercial center of the sorts of the erstwhile capital of a great and more like nation of Red men. The final stages of our journey on the Missouri was to Council Bluffs where we found to our surprise and delight that the big brother of waters was readily navigable from there to Sioux City, and set forth post haste in our tiny craft.

Our first birdseye vision of the city, in all fairness, was a disappointment. We expected to see some enchanted village of teepees with open campfires. In contrast, what we saw was amazingly like Kansas City on an infinitely smaller scale. We proceeded, nevertheless, down a dark street until we came upon what appeared to be a shop in which numerous articles were displayed for sale. My eye was caught by a queer design suspended above the door. Three Guild-colored spheres dangled, arranged in a sort of arc, and noting an announcement directly underneath which informed me that the shopkeepers also bought articles of merchandise. I was determined to submit my proposition to trade the boat for a sled and dog team. We entered the place when the merchant came forward to help us. He was short in stature, rather stoutish about the girth, and no part of the face was not covered by a thick beard. Inside whiskers seemed much lighter than the complexion we associated with him. The clothes he wore were somewhat shabby with a suit of darkish cloth, and his feet were clad with soft slippers which appeared to be made of canvas. His head was covered completely by a black cloth cap which fit snugly on his cranium. Astonished, I was taken aback by an odor, not unlike that of an ordinary onion, but much more penetrating which he appeared to emit upon opening a door leading, no doubt to his domestic quarters. I glanced, not without some misgivings, to my husband who answered by whispering that perhaps he belonged to that strange race of which our guide spoke so often. I was determined to make a close examination of this creature as might be, without giving offense. Upon scrutinizing him more closely I saw what I had not at first noticed, the most peculiar thing about his physiognomy. His nose, the slide was of enormous proportions with a decided bell from tip to base. I could scarcely restrain my exclamation of unconcealed astonishment, the same being narrowly averted when the man put to us the question in a tongue we could not understand. Then, in a moment, a voice from whence the odor had come, called out with a strange braying sound. "Bubba! Oh Bubba, "we are looking for an exchange," if I properly understood her. The man, I assumed an Indian now, raised his arms with a quick gesture that suggested he had a weapon, and without any more discussion, we turned and fled. The Indian followed us out onto the street shouting and gesticulating in a manner that convinced us that he meant to do us harm. But we really did not know!

Having put no thought as to the direction we ran, we arrived at the intersection of what appeared to be a principal thoroughfare. Pausing there from sheer lack of breath, we noted with dismay that what the guide had told us about the commercialization of Sioux City was true indeed. Bearing directly towards us came one of the streetcars we had thought we left behind in Kansas City. True it was of smaller dimensions than the ones to which we had been used. I believe it was called the

Rockinghorse type. To our amazement was the lighting from the car which showed off specimens of what must surely have been another race. There was a male and a female who were not red as we had thought that the Sioux would be but the color of chocolate as they came near, we noted that the lips were abnormally large and the protruding noses were not the size or shape of the irate shopkeeper.

Completely bewildered we pressed up the street to locate some friendly white people who could speak our tongue. It was to no avail. Hundreds of people passed but all bore the physical resemblance of either the shopkeeper or the brown couple although they were varying shades of pigment and length. We determined to make our camp in the nearby open country and to quit this unfriendly city the following morning. The weather was still fair, and we hoped to proceed further without the use of dogs. As we plowed on to battle our way into South Dakota it became clear to us, with every step we took, why the Scandinavian people had been described in the history of all peoples as the slowest, most deliberative, of all races. But enough of this, we needed to solve the baffling problem of locomotion. We timed ourselves only to discover to our dismay that it took just exactly 2 hours and 56 minutes to take a step into Vermillion, South Dakota. To add to a general alarm it became apparent that once that step was taken, it was not a stepping into progress but rather it became apparent when that step was once taken was a step that threw us back to the place where we had started.

To finally get there, we used our ropes and pulleys to advantage, to say nothing of sticks of dynamite, to climb away from there. We planted our feet firmly in the 9-foot snowbanks to prevent sinking over our heads. We would hastily stampede on the snow when we found firm packs beneath us. After that, we more or less found ourselves over our heads in many ways. We frequently said that we would survey the situation and decide whether the pulley would be the thing or whether we'd be forced to resort to dynamite. Then we blasted and dug away through to the next stopping place or pulled and dug ourselves up over an embankment to repeat the procedure one more time. This method of marching had many disadvantages. We were often forced to stop, so it made it take longer and longer than what we had been told was the usual two hours and 56 minutes. We often checked for frozen fingers and toes, to say nothing of taking time out to cover or remove ears. But the outstanding disaster of the trip came on the third morning. I was arguing with the guide as to the best method of cooking griddle cakes. It must be remembered that we were using dynamite to our advantage, and Lars was insisting that the griddle cakes should be tossed into the air, allowing them to alight in the pan. "You thickheaded fool," I shouted, "you run the risk when you throw the pancakes in the air, rather than just turn them, that they will take a dive into the snow, and then we are virtually sure of having no breakfast. You gamble when you throw it in the air, granted, Lars, and he taught me to throw it in the air." I acquiesced into pleasantries but that was about the most you seemed to contribute to our general progress on this trip, was that skull of yours too thick to comprehend that the cakes cooked just the same way with the throwing up or turned over with a gentle guiding hand and force them to remain in the pan where we wanted them. Suddenly, Lars, our guide, turned around and jumped over the embankment, and he was gone. We looked around to discover that he was looking for a new tourist and that he was abandoning us.

For what seemed like 18 days, we were blown along the Novascandilouvia territory as a mighty Gale storm, with the force of a cyclone, hit us. We took out the guidebook and consulted it when the north wind continued during these months: August, September, October, November, December, January, February, March, April, and May. I continued reading South Winds continued during June and July. Why must this be the wind the guidebook mentions? We decided to spread the tent like a sail, we fastened it securely, grasped the ridge pole, and away we skimmed, blown over the crusty snow like two huge birds. Did the wind always blow like this always I inquired later. Yes, I believe it was reported to never cease!

Unaware, we flew further and further into this tundra. Little did we realize that we had already seen and experienced all there was to see and experience in South Dakota. The blowing wind was the only exciting thing that ever seemed to happen in this territory, except for the weather. This gave the natives something to look forward to so that they could expect a change every day and sometimes twice a day. Everything in South Dakota was always blowing about. Never did rain or snow descend from the sky without the accompaniment of wind. Neither did the inhabitants ever attempt accomplishments of any kind, without the same sense of blowing of air. Whatever happened or was predicted to happen, the wind howled and shrieked. Days may come and days may go, but the wind blew on forever. Once we landed, I remarked that I had seen no new people. Where do you suppose the people are? Perhaps they'd all been scalped, Johnny said. "You are mistaken," a deep voice to my left advised. We turned startled to discover a huge American Indian person sailing along by our sides. "You are mistaken," he repeated. "We Sioux feel ourselves deeply indebted to the white man for having taken this land off our hands. This land is such a liability that the Scandinavians have tried several times to return this territory to us, but we will not take it, no, never." Then he grew so fierce, showing his bad teeth. "We will kill them if they don't keep this godforsaken land."

"But what is the matter with the land?" I inquired.

He finished with, " May you someday make your escape." As he bid us goodbye, he cautioned us now to remember that new ideas were taboo, smuggling in magazines from the outside taboo, thoughts of leaving this territory taboo, just did not go about prying into other people's business, and you would get along as well as can be expected. Whatever you did, see that you do not amuse yourself with any sort of artistic or intellectual occupation. We thanked him, looked at each other, and went forward.

The area we were in has been home to Native American tribes for centuries. French fur traders first visited in the late 18th century. Vermillion was founded in 1859 and incorporated in 1873. It was also populated by Norwegian and German people. From October to April, it went below 0 degrees Fahrenheit, and some days in winter as low as 22 degrees below. The highest it went when we were there was 75 degrees, but those days were few, and since we were only there for the academic year, it meant that most of the time it was freezing. The academic year was from September to early May, so we rarely saw a nice warm day. The original town was entirely below the bluffs on the banks of the Missouri River, and three-quarters of it washed away in the 1811 Great Flood. Now, it froze over when it didn't flood, and sometimes it flooded and then froze. And then there were the Glacier lakes that were just north of us. The town had some Queen Anne-style houses, a well-constructed Renaissance revival building, as well as a colonial building, in the little town that was used for the University. Offices and classes were held in this building. There was also an old armory on the campus and a Gothic Revival church. The downtown, which was really just a block and a half, offered little except necessary supplies. There was a bank, a feed store, a courthouse, and a variety store. There was a small library in town, but having no means to get there, I often had to rely on Johnny to get me a book. Similarly, newspapers were very hard to get.

We lived near Spirit Mound, or Paha Wakan, about seven miles north of Vermillion, the highest point in Clay County. Although there were other hills nearby, the mound was striking in its relative isolation. Geologists called this kind of formation a Roche Moutonée, a bedrock knob that was shaped but not leveled by the last Pleistocene glacier between 10,000 and 13,000 years ago. Before arriving in this area, Lewis & Clark had heard that the local Omaha, Oto, and Yankton tribes believed the mound to be occupied by little spirits with "remarkably large heads" who shot any human who came near.

The little Georgian house we lived in, way outside of the Town of Vermillon, was owned by a deaf woman, and so I had no one else to talk to all day, every day. We were unable to rent other rooms. Our room was very small, and we were too far from town or the University for me to go anywhere. On the occasional day when the sun was out in the winter, I would venture across the frozen tundra. A bicycle would not work on ice, and in the frigid cold, dog sleds would have been a better idea, but we did not have access to any. Often, I just sat, too depressed to even write. Once we were safely back in the civilized world, which we had so foolishly forsaken for the sake of adventure, the whole experience seemed like a ghastly nightmare. I was still so close to it, too close to forget the awful realities, the bitter cold, the primitive people, the unbelievable story of it all, that we had now, without reluctance, been persuaded to set down here as the strange tale, careful to omit nothing for the readers.

We went on for months as it became increasingly clear to us that a country that couldn't climatically support flowers or trees or shrubs could never hope to maintain a race of people very far in advance of the animal stage. Neither could people live for nine months with the only idea being how to fill their stomachs and provide their bodies with heat against the ravages of blizzard winds. How could they hope to evolve to a much higher plane than that? We spent our days listening to the native tales of how they had put outsiders in their place. We heard of lynchings and torture that were committed on persons of all types, especially antagonizing the Scandalovians. They told of atrocities committed by the legislature upon the people, especially upon those connected with the state university, which the legislature body was most desirous of stamping out because it instilled a dangerous influence in the spreading of progressive propaganda. They called it a nuisance as regards instilling ideas of refinement and culture in the minds of the youth of this territory.

A Scandinavian re-counted to us the story of a South Dakota legislature, which after three special sessions, was required to cut the appropriations of the state university and then discovered to its dismay that none of the professors would teach for half pay except for one from the Ku Klux Klan who was driven out of Texas. And Johnny didn't realize that he, too, was teaching at half pay. But I digress from my purpose to describe a method of procedure to get through this wasteland.

One day, a friend from Sioux City smuggled in a copy of the New York Times. We pounced on it equally anxious to learn what the World War I had brought and who had won or lost. That information was denied to us. We had no idea if it had been settled one way or another. We had no idea what country we were now a citizen of, and what had happened in the world over the last few months. Then, with a characteristic outspokenness, I flung back my head and decided that we could go on no longer. I was suffering to the breaking point. Cautiously, we pulled down the shades and prepared for an orgy. First, we brought out a few dog-eared and tattered magazines and books that our friend from Sioux City had lent us, and we pulled out cigarettes, and not without misgivings, lit them. Our strength was fast failing us, and we were forced to take this risk. We just settled back in our chairs, miraculously enjoying our sins openly smoking, drinking, and other immoral non-conformist things that perhaps are leading this country to destruction. "Hush, is there anything to drink?"

"Be quiet about it, hurry before we have to destroy the evidence and need to lie about it."

The wind whipped up again, and an Indian friend said, "You see the spare spot pointing to a place where the snow hit to form a 20-foot embankment, that is what this wind does to South Dakota. The land is all like that, the crops blown out of the ground and over into Iowa as fast as they are planted."

"But surely there is something in life besides crops."

"Not in South Dakota," he replied, and as the kind Indian said grimly, we had found his statement to be true and characteristically correct. We had been in South Dakota for three months, living as we had since we found it. We had no semblance of a real life other than traces of the American Indians we found friendly and people occasionally encountered at the University.

We were finally able to get a dog and sled so that we could get around. The country had been laid out for us as it had been for generations, flat, monotonous. We needed to believe in our hearts that it was possible for a place to contain life, and we had read in the guidebooks that it did. Before we departed from Kansas City, we had ascertained from four sources, of two other bands of adventuresome explorers who had once upon a time left the world behind and ventured into the wilds of the Dakotas, although they had never returned or been heard of since. Never returned or been heard of since. The words rang in my head until I thought I should go mad. Johnny just yelled at the dogs, and we were suddenly in a brisk argument. "We must find some signs of habitation or I shall go crazy." I wrapped up in as many layers as I could, took the dogs, put a pen and paper in my bag, and went outside. "Perhaps we can find some traces of civilization," I said hopelessly. Let's try to do something. Hopefully, this country of the Sioux surely has some arrowheads in the next clear space. We can at least commence to search for remnants of the Sioux Indians." We traveled and stopped at a clearing. I was digging around in the snow with my trusty pickaxe when I screamed. Over on the other side of the dog sled, I found a flat head sticking up near the spiritual mountain of large heads. Johnny ran to my side and discovered to my amazement that I had found the top of a head lying in the snow. It was a clearly defined flat head, but was it an arrowhead? It did not seem pointed enough. With our pickaxes and shovels, we commenced frantically to disembody it from the snow. We worked away for three hours, but still, it seemed to be buried very deep in the snow and ice. I demanded that we use excessive caution when uncovering the head, as you never know when you're excavating something, or what's there. Maybe it's an Icelandic mummy?" We didn't know what we were uncovering. Alas, we kept digging for two days and three nights. On the third day, we removed a mummy from its snowy resting place, we wrapped him up in a bear skin on the sled. I was wrapping the last bearskin around him when I said, "Let's see how hard he is. I will just try sticking this hatpin in him." Johnny noted, "He's already past repair, but do not stick the poor helpless creature with a hat pin, it's not fair to him."

"Yes, but I want to see how hard he is," and I thrust the pin in hard, and as far as I could into the thick, closed abdomen. Imagine our shock when we saw the mummy open his blue eyes and give a massive yowl, jump up, and do three somersaults in the air, lighting at last upon the hat pin. I ran to him and extracted it, in my best offhand manner while he sat up on his haunches crying excessive tears, which froze and bounced off onto the ground. "Oh, I beg your pardon, sir, as I contritely gathered the bear robes which were now strewn on the snow. We queried the mummy, who was apparently coming to. "I'm ever so sorry, really," I said as I methodically placed the robes up on the sled. "Where am I?" he bore a strange resemblance to our former guide, Lars Jensen. He gazed about the surrounding landscape and then lapsed into a state of coma. This lasted for perhaps eight hours. In the meantime, Johnny and I made a careful examination of the specimen's genus homo. He was obviously from South Dakota; his head, as I mentioned, was flat and did not seem to function. His eyes were blue, his cheeks were red, and his hair was a dirty color. He was short and stocky, and the few sounds which had escaped from his mouth had resembled a donkey bray and a pig's grunt. About his face, he wore the unmistakable odor provided by the atmosphere. It threw off a decidedly fishy stench. His habits that we had witnessed over the eight hours of sitting with him were apathetic, pitifully unimaginative. The explanation of his condition, we later discovered, was to be found in the continuing battle of the elements which the Scandeluvians (part German and part Scandinavian, as we later learned to call him) necessarily endured.

After some eight hours of immobility, our Scandinavian mummy roared and stretched himself. He regarded us with impassive, expressionless face, "Well maybe spring be here vot?"

"What makes you think so?" I asked, glancing about at the snowy landscape stretching away in every direction. "I'd be out asserted Hans Hansen," which was his name. "Oh, that's only because we've dug you out," we replied.

"Do you mean you've been snowbound all winter and never once been out?"

"Snowed in September," answered Hans, "must be May now."

"God no, this is only March."

"But March, huh, then I go back in," and he started to climb back into the hole.

"Hold on, wait a minute, when will you be back out again?"

Hans lingered. "Maybe May, if the snow melts," and he disappeared into his hole again, everything was as before we talked all over that night before we turned into our tent. For the natives of Nova Scandinavia, it seemed that they buried themselves for the winter, and then came out in May like the flowers after the melting of the snow. That was a short time to live out in the world. June, July, maybe August, which possibly accounted for some of the rumors we'd heard, that we couldn't wait till May for them to come out. I begged for Johnny to lower me into Hans' hole, and with misgivings, he followed. We found that it wasn't as cold as we had expected. This was what one called being in a state of refrigeration. We went all the way down into the hole, and merrily we discovered that we were in a tiny city with narrow winding streets in a strange space with two-story houses. We trenched about the lonely, deserted sidewalks and gazed at the buildings and houses for three hours without finding any semblance of civilization. Suddenly, just as we turned a sharp corner, we fell upon a tiny remnant of the outside world, a tattered bookcase! This we eagerly examined, believing that it might just have something that matters, but we found to our dismay that most of the pages of the books on the shelves had been torn out. Chagrined to have been so near a discovery, only to find that we were hopeless. What shall we do? "We must find the owner of the bookcase, of course." Faster and faster we paced through bleak streets, our eyes alert for further clues. At last, I dropped from sheer exhaustion upon the snow, my hands were numb from the cold, and my heart had become an icicle. We weren't getting anywhere, which I had frequently observed about Scandinavia. Johnny's heart had truly become an icicle also, and I noted that our sensibilities were numb. "Come on, let's leave this land of frozen dreams," I said, "Let us speed back to civilization at once after we find out the source of the bookcase." Johnny said, "I will stay here until I uncover the secrets of this country's destitution or die."

"Well, we shall both be dead tomorrow anyway at this rate," I declared, "there isn't much longer to suffer." At this juncture, we were startled by the crackling of icicles behind us. "Pardon me," said a kind voice, but I overheard your last remark. "Believe me, I pity you and your plight, and I will do whatever I can to be a friend to you."

"Who are you?" I asked this beautiful, dark-haired stranger.

"Oh, you need not worry, I am not from this territory, as you may observe by my coloring and the texture of my skin." Although his skin did resemble leather. But he did not look like the other indigenous people that we had met.

"I came to this country from the outside world." He turned to wipe a tear before it froze in his eyelash.

"But why did you not return to the world?"

"I could not find my way out, I was frozen in my tracks, lost, in a maze," he said. "Have you ever heard of anyone from this world coming to explore NovaScandinouvia and being allowed to return with tales of what he saw? No, there is a reason they never allow foreigners, as they call them, to return. It would bring too much ridicule and contempt from the world upon them."

"Do you mean that we can never go back to Kansas City?"

"Not if they find you," the stranger said. He came over to me, and with me in a flash, I remembered what so many of our intellectual friends had said to us in Kansas City.

"Is there no way out?" I bemoaned.

"Not from South Dakota," the stranger said.

"What shall we do, what shall we do?"

"Quick, come with me," the stranger said, and we ducked into a snow hut just in time to observe a Scandilouvian in a little wheeled sled who had hopped out from behind one of the box-like houses unexpectedly. The Scandilouvian lowered his glance toward our snowy huts with a characteristic suspiciousness, giving us his blank wooden visage, his only semblance of expression. Then he stopped slowly to pick up another chip, which he had added to the collection on his shoulder as he moved on, deliberately grunting as he walked down the street. "You'll have to disguise yourself," the stranger told us as he helped us to make a rapid change into red flannels, dirty overworld black caps with your tabs, and heavy sweaters. He then handed us each a pair of mittens, "Do not let them know in any way that you were from the outside world and pretend you've lived here always, then perhaps." Then it seemed that the man who had come from behind the house and two other people started running towards us. We ran away and ran towards the hole to try to find our dog sled. As we climbed out, we hurriedly hoisted the tent. They had almost reached us when, in an angry fright, they grabbed at the ridge pole and then shouted out for our salvation. The wind seemed to have heard us and gained more than its usual impetus, lifted us. Clutching with all our might at our tent, it lifted higher and grazed off the ground and flopped like a Satanic sail, bidding farewell to the free, open tundra. I gritted my teeth and lifted my heels off the ground and out of the snow. I watched gloriously as we were sent up, up and up. We saw them below until we were far above Mount Hernia, and we were one with the clouds of the sky. I asked, "Where do we go from here?"

Johnny just replied, "Anywhere, anywhere but back there."

And that was the story for our adventure into that undiscovered territory about which so much had been conjectured and so little really ascertained. We believe that those notes were the only extensive information concerning the countryside and its inhabitants. We were convinced that we were the only explorers alive who had weathered its hardships and returned to our homes alive. We had written the story about it as a warning to other fearless souls who might, in moments of ambitious planning, rashly propose to penetrate these wild spaces. Let our experiences quell your enthusiasm for such a project, and let our narrow escape be your lesson. We decided that whatever we did next, it had to be where there was a city, preferably Paris.

Although we never thought that Paris could be more dangerous, the Paris that I then went to afterward was the Paris of German Occupation. Now, I wished that I could just fly out of the Paris that I was now in, fly on a parachute tent, or find an underground tunnel back home. But I was here in Paris, along with a small boy and a dog, isolated as if I were back in the Dakotas, cold, without heat, most of the time without electricity, without a guide, or even a friendly Scandinavian face.

By December 1939, even canned foods were scarce in Paris. No oil was to be found. The only vegetables were from someone's garden, or if they had canned something. Finally, in late January, I decided that Bobby and I had to travel south as the doctor had previously recommended. Earlier, in the summer, I had gone to the American Embassy, and they told me that if I wanted to leave for America, I needed to go to Bordeaux and stay in the little fishing village of Arcachon. When I was finally well enough to leave, I gathered a few cans of "cassoulets," cans of beans with pork or ham. I bought many cans over the past few months to have in an emergency. There was also some rice and noodles. I gave them to a French mom who had a young son and said Au Revoir as I prepared to go, ultimately to Lisbon, where I could then set Sail for America. But we first had to travel to Bordeaux to get our papers. I had not heard from Johnny or received any money from him or the press for months. Perhaps, when I get to Bordeaux, I could have some funds wired to me. Perhaps when we got to Bordeaux, everything would be alright. If we could get there?

Chapter 7
Brass

When you don't have any food, you become desperate and it becomes the most important thing. How carefully I used to pack up jars and cans and food for travel. When Johnny and I had left Vermillion South Dakota we had decided that whatever we did next it had to be where there was a city, preferably Paris. We thought that in Paris we would never have isolation, starvation, or cold. We thought that Paris represented civilization. We had not yet had a honeymoon so whatever happened it would be our honeymoon. Johnny knew how miserable I was in South Dakota so when he was offered a position in Paris, this time by the *NY Herald Tribune*, we jumped at the opportunity. What an incredible opportunity to live in Paris rather than Vermillion South Dakota. We were off on our adventure but to NYC and then Paris. We had saved some money and decided that our honeymoon would consist of hitchhiking across the states to NYC so that we could then get to Paris from there. We didn't have a car or the money to pay for a train to go that far, so hitchhiking seemed like the logical solution.

Hitchhiking had become popular in the 1920s as the automobile became more common and highways stretched from one end of the United States to the other. Everyone was talking about J.K. Christian of Chicago, who had traveled over 3,000 miles in less than a month by asking motorists for "lifts."[18] It was also reported in the New York Times that a student at the Yale School of Forestry, Delzie Demaree, had "used his thumb to get rides from Arkansas to New Haven, Connecticut for a total cost of 29 cents." They started calling it hitchhiking. I shared the idea with Johnny, and he loved it. We were off. We packed as little as possible so that we could carry it. One bag would need to be for food. I spent the last day in South Dakota excitedly running about, reducing all of my belongings to one suitcase. I didn't have much more than that anyway. My beige suitcase with brown trim was old and worn, so I was so excited when Becca, my big sister, gave me a new suitcase for the trip. Now Johnny and I would each have one. We fit most of our clothing in one suitcase and put sandwiches that I made in the other with some cans of spam, a loaf of bread, some cereal, smoked fish, and cookies that I made a few days before. We each had a canteen for water. We were ready to go.

We waited on the side of the road now to see how far we could travel. Most days we were picked up within an hour, sometimes it took 10 minutes, and one time we waited on a deserted road for

---

[18] "3023 Miles by Auto 'Lifts'", New York Times, Oct 31, 1921

3 hours. It certainly helped that I was there. People were not used to seeing a nicely dressed woman looking for a ride on the side of the road. Based on what we read, we calculated that we could make it to NYC in a month. It was 1,325 miles from Vermillion, South Dakota, to Times Square. We calculated that if we could do at least 50 miles a day, we could make it in 30 days.

Our first real stop would be Denver, Colorado. I had worked there and knew people, Betty's mother lived there, and we spent the night at her home. Betty's mother tried to give us some money to take a train, but we told her that this was our honeymoon adventure.

We spent the first part of the next ride sitting on hay in the back of a pick-up truck, watching the sights of Colorado pass us by. A couple of hours outside of Denver, we saw the red rocks, which seemed to erupt from the cracked and sometimes dusty basin. As the light shifted, we could see purple hues as if they were painted on the rocks, pinks merged with patches of green grass and shrubs. The next part of the trip took us past soaring silos, farmlands with hay neatly piled up. We were dropped off at the feed store, where we found our next ride. Just before we entered Kansas, past the elevated plains of Colorado and more familiar territory, we saw a large brand-new carousel being built. The driver told us that it would go 12 miles per hour. We wanted to go on it, but with all our possessions in hand and our time frame, it just wasn't possible. So, we travelled on. The scenery changed from low mountains to rolling hills, to flat wheatfields and endless roads, passing small towns along the way. Twelve hours and three rides later, we were back in Lawrence, Kansas, where we could visit family before going off on our NYC to Paris sojourn. It was great to take a nice bath and fill up our basket with some fresh food to take on the next part of our trip.

I was so glad we did because our next "hitched" ride only took us to St Louis, Missouri, and we realized that we were off the Lincoln Highway. We had to get back on track and find a ride north. We were dropped off in a shanty town area along the river. I was terrified, but the people were very nice. They obviously had very few worldly possessions, but the children seemed happy playing in the only world that they knew. We did not want to impose on anyone. It was a nice night, and we took the blanket that we had with us and found a nice soft spot in the woods to spend the night. Johnny lit a fire. His time in the military helped with our camping out, and I was in awe as he found wood, built a fire, got some fresh water from the stream, and dug a little trench around our blanket. As I lay there, I thought that I had never seen so many stars. It was beautiful to lie in Johnny's arms in the fresh air by a big tree. The stars were twinkling, and I could hear the water rushing from a stream nearby. A part of me wanted to just stay in that spot forever with my love, my protector, my slayer of dragons. At that moment, I was truly his Princess. The grass beneath our blanket was our kingdom. Life was so simple then.

It was easy the next morning to get a ride from St Louis to Chicago, Illinois. So many cars were going that way, and we told them that we had jobs there. They were each very accommodating. We were finally back on the Highway and two-thirds of the way to NYC. We now rode through the night on a 16-hour trek to NYC. Ben, who drove us this last leg, was happy to have the company and asked Johnny to drive part of the way so that he could sleep. We stopped by the side of the road, and we shared the remainder of our sandwiches, which we brought from Kansas, with Ben. We drove into NYC just as the sun was rising, and I was so excited to see the buildings and movement of the city as everyone began their day. Ben dropped us off by the New York Herald office, but we decided to find a nearby rooming house so that Johnny could get washed up and dressed nicely for his new boss. We had made sure that we saved enough for the rooming house in NYC, although it cost much more than we had planned. We were so excited when the Herald said that they could provide a room for us before our boat left the following week. We had made it in less than 30 days, in plenty of time, and it only cost us $5, well, at least until we got to NYC.

It was the longest time that Johnny and I had ever spent together. It was beautiful to talk in person and not write letters. I lay in his arms when I got tired, and we met interesting people along the way. It was the roaring twenties, and everyone was so hopeful about prospects. In NYC, there was music in the streets, and one night we spent too much money and went to a dance hall. Most other nights, I would go to the store and pick up food that we could eat in our little room so that we could save our money. I put a blanket on the floor, and each meal was a picnic adventure. We laughed and kissed and told stories. We didn't know which stories were real and which were made up. Our life together was truly beginning, and our next stop was Paris!

Johnny and I journeyed to France full of ambitions and dreams. The steamship made the journey in about 5 days, and it was beautiful. The Herald had booked us on the fastest ship at the time. We were, of course, not in the first-class area, but we snuck up there one day and we walked tap the long deck looking out at the ocean. As we pulled into the French port, a full moon lit up the tiny village of Le Havre, France. Before heading into Paris, we strolled the medieval streets with their huge ramparts. They were illuminated as they held back the sea on all sides. Here, we watched waves booming in, moonlight touching the sloping roofs of small houses, and all about them the immense sea and sky. We felt like we were the only two in the universe right then. Johnny would carry on about how beautiful I looked in my deep blue suit and describe my eyes as deep pools of blue water. He never seemed to tire of putting me on a pedestal, then.

Once in Paris, we found a perfect place to stay near the Boulevard St Germain. It was the Hotel D'Orsay, and full of beautiful antique furnishings. It had been a house for a nobleman who had lived there when the court was at the Louvre. We were just across the river from the Louvre, while the École de Beaux-Arts was exactly behind us. An English woman with half-French parentage ran it, so we had good food and wonderful talks. There was an adorable living room with a bed and dressing room, and our meals were $2.60 a day, for both of us.

Whenever we could take a day to travel somewhere, we did. We would take a train, or a bus, or find a ride. Our travels extended to all over France and to Rome, Italy. I studied French and wrote down recipes of all the great food, whether it was an omelet or an entrée in Alsace. But reality struck when we were suddenly called back to the States. One day, without warning, the newspaper told Johnny that they needed him back in NYC, and we had to leave immediately. I was so disappointed. I just wanted to stay in Europe forever. I tried to convince Johnny to speak to the Herald and other newspapers. I begged and cried, but I think that he was ready to go home. I was not. I never wanted to leave, but alas, fairy tales cannot go on forever. I swore that I would get back to Paris as soon as I could.

We had no idea why they were recalling him back, but without a job, a source of income, and someone paying for the apartment, we had no choice but to return immediately on the ship that they had booked us on. It was strange that it was so immediate, and that the only one available was to Boston. This ship also now takes 11 days and not 5, as before. What was happening in NY that our journey had to end so abruptly? We had no idea that it was the impending doom across the country that perhaps the newspapers knew about before anyone else, but said nothing to us.

As soon as I knew that we would be back in NYC, I reached out to my contacts and was very quickly offered a job. One newspaper told me that I would have the job as soon as I arrived, as long as I had two articles to hand in once I arrived: one on Paris styles, and one on French cooking. I was so excited, but perhaps the stress took over before we could leave, and I had an appendicitis attack while still in Paris. I came to realize that I had had this problem for years, but they took out my appendix at the

American Hospital in Paris. I had no time to write the two articles. I was determined to write it on the ship as we sailed back to NYC. I stayed in the room and wrote away. Johnny would bring me food, and we would go for a stroll on the deck in the morning. I thought that Paris was the best time of my life, and all I dreamed of was to return. But we returned to Boston and then took a train to New York on September 21. Just one month later, the stock market crashed, and all of NYC abruptly changed. My job was soon cut, and my fantasy world of Paris and of being a writer would come to an abrupt end. It seems that the realities of life always interrupt our fantasies.

My fantasy dream of returning to Paris one day was now a nightmare. I was finally back in Paris a decade later (well, actually a suburb of Paris), but I was alone and desperately hungry.

The last apartment to vacate in our Meudon building was a French woman with an Alsacian husband (who now worked for the Germans). She soon left as well. My article from just a few years earlier seemed pointless. So much for the blending of races.

For three days, before the Germans arrived on our block, I watched day and night, people streaming up the hill past our door. They were pushing their belongings in baby carriages, wheeling bicycles, using a wheelbarrow, or carrying packs on their back, often loaded up with suitcases in one hand and a child in the other. Cars and taxis were piled high with personal belongings. Beds were strapped to the roof of the car. Dogs, birds, and cats peered out from cramped car windows. They rolled, walked, and crawled past our window. The people who had horses with carts filled with their belongings were the lucky ones because the cars were soon running out of gas. Other people leaving were on bicycles with everything they could strapped to the bike and their backs. Little children were also carrying not just a suitcase but the weight of the world on their shoulders. They were scared, and they whimpered and cried. Everyone was leaving, but where would they go? They often walked for hours, for days, with only a few crusts of bread and some sardines or smoked meat for as long as it might last. Some were sick already and could barely walk. I saw an old man sitting on the sidewalk across the street. He sat there for hours until he fell over. He never got up again. He was just left there, and the smell of rotting flesh filled the air that once smelled of roses and lilacs.

The only person that I knew who was still there on the block was a Janitress in the building across the street who was waiting for her French soldier/husband to return. Her son Renee was Bobby's only friend now. Bobby seemed so worried about her that I went with the two children across the street to check up on Renee and her baby. As I walked in, she suddenly burst out, "You must go, Madame… mother of Bobby…to Paris on your bicycle. (We didn't even know each other's names at that point). It was only seven miles. The railroads are not running, and there are no automobiles. The Germans have taken all of the gasoline. You can make it. You have a good bicycle. You must go every day as long as you can get past the sentries. You must take the side streets. I can tell you how. I will watch Bobby and the dog." She continued, "When you are in Paris, you will surely find one or two open shops. There you can buy food for the five of us. Everything that you can fit in your basket." Sitting there warm and cozy on her featherbed, she motioned for all the children to come and sit with her. "Tell the shopkeepers that you are buying food for a French woman who has 5 children, 11, whatever you want. I am all alone. Tell them that my husband was at the Ligne Maginot. Tell them that you are going home to America as soon as you can, but first, you must find some food for me. Tell them that I am starving!" She stopped, exhausted, and lay back on the bed. "Now, please get whatever you can. I haven't many centuries left. Buy whatever you find that is cheap. Madame bought all the egg noodles and evaporated or powdered milk; all that you can possibly persuade them to let you have." I was out the door and yelled back, "Bobby, stay here with Renee. Please listen to his mother and DO NOT leave the apartment, please," she yelled back, "You might find some powdered milk at the pharmacies."

Luckily, I had bought a bicycle when I first arrived, in anticipation of a country vacation. Now there was scarcely a bicycle to be seen. Not a single car. The streets were completely deserted, not one living French soul, only German troops on the main boulevards. The fear was ringing in my ears and made me feel sick and weak. I thought I couldn't do this, but I had to. I got off the bicycle and walked for a while. As I rode onto the streets of Paris, I could still see the Notre Dame Cathedral, but realized that I was ignoring every usual landmark as I only looked for open shops, cafes, and pharmacies. A loaf of bread from one shop, egg noodles from another. My story got better as I went to each shop, convincing the shop owner to sell me something. The pharmacy had powdered milk for sale. One shop had lard for cooking. Every day after that, I trudged to Paris and the three adjoining towns to find a single radish and a few leaves of lettuce. Another would let me buy some damaged cans that no longer had a label. I had no idea what was in them and didn't care. I filled the basket with as much as I could and headed back, hoping that I was not too lost. Every day, I began this journey. I would buy all the food that I could, even if I had previously considered it not palatable. I had to make my money last. My money was supposed to come twice a month from Johnny and the *UPI* and *Herald Tribune* via American Express. But the American Express office had closed, and I had no idea when I would get any more. Luckily, I have always been frugal and saved as much money as I could. There were very few places to spend it anyway. For six months, I had received no letters, cables, or monies. I had a few thousand francs saved up and wore them morning, noon, and night in a money belt. Eventually, American Express opened a little office in a town outside of Paris, which I would ride to once a week to get cables, money, and letters. There was some money from the Herald, but nothing from Johnny.

Each day, I went to look for food, going to another part of the inner city of Paris. The city that had so mesmerized me a decade earlier now only existed for finding food. One day, I was stopped by a German officer, but I spoke French very quickly, showed him my Press Pass, and gave him a loaf of bread. Thereafter, I took some of the flowers that I found and made cookies beautifully wrapped. I gave them to German soldiers when they stopped me, or shopkeepers who gave me a hard time. And every once in a while, there would be a person who had been shot in the middle of the street, just left there to rot and die. The first time I went to the side of the road and vomited, but as it became more frequent, I became immune to the sight and the smell of a dead body. I eventually just kept on riding past them, hardly noticing if it was a man or a woman, young or old.

How we survived those next few months, I don't know. Who would have thought that a can of condensed milk would cost $5 in 1940? It was great that Laurencia, Renee's mother (now I knew her name), and I knew how to make wonderful things to eat out of nothing. I picked berries in an empty lot and made jam with a little bit of sugar that I could find from an open café. Apples that I picked from a tree at a park became a wonderful applesauce, aided by a little cinnamon stick that I still had left. I spent month after month after month with every minute spent collecting food, cooking, and trying to give our children a little bit of normalcy that would replace the hunger in their bellies. One day, Bobby and Renee went into the woods and came back with school bags and backpacks filled with chestnuts. We cooked and ate chestnuts in every conceivable form for the next six weeks. Chestnut soup was made by pureeing the chestnuts and adding water so it would go further, and if I had found a little piece of salted bacon, it would make it very flavorful and filling. When we could not find egg noodles, we could grind up the chestnuts into a flour paste, shape them into thick ribbons, and after they dried, we could boil them to make pasta. Chestnuts also went great with squash or mushrooms, if we could find any. We were always a little wary of picking the mushrooms in the nearby woods. We could also just boil or roast the chestnuts to eat straight when the stomach pangs of hunger were bad. Of course, there was always Marons Glace, which was like candy. We would occasionally make this little treat as a bonus for the children. You simply dunk the chestnuts into a sugary syrup (so that you don't need much sugar), let them soak for a few days, and then dry them in the oven.

But as much as we tried to keep the children from being scared or wanting to go outside to play, there would be many bad days. The days got worse. The fear and the hunger never subsided. Occasionally, Renee would ask when his father was coming home. Renee began to ask more frequently about his father and would whimper and cry at night. They never did see him again. Eventually, Laurencia decided that she had to leave. They left Meudon. Now Bobby and I and Mitzie were truly on our own, alone, isolated, scared, and hungry.

In Meudon, I kept hearing stories about people in the town who didn't have enough to eat. People were literally starving and dying. There was this one old gentleman of perhaps 80. He shuffled down the street in a beige smock. He looked at me one day and said that the stores would open in a month, maybe two at the most. "Don't worry," he said. Weeks later, someone told me that he was now very ill and alone. Some others and I brought him whatever we could and sat with him. It was bad enough to be hungry, but he was also so lonely. I was afraid of seeing people lying in the street dying of starvation. In the summer months, food was scarce, but by September and October, there were absolutely no fresh fruits or vegetables to be found anywhere.

I knew that it was going to be a very long winter. Ever since July, we found practically no nourishment in the shops or the markets. There were shortages of all kinds. There were no blankets, bath towels, ordinary brown wrapping paper, soap of any kind, no pens, pencils, hairpins, gloves, or stockings. All this, along with the real tragedy of shortages of meat, butter, cheese, eggs, noodles, potatoes, rice, cereal, or any kind of fruit. A few vegetables were occasionally grown in someone's yard, and on a rare occasion, there was fish. I continued my journey for food, but there was no milk; I occasionally found a beer. I drank the beer, but I think it made me ill. I lay in bed sick and vomiting for days, thinking it was the beer, but it could have just been the malnutrition. Perhaps beer does not do well on a swollen, empty belly.

One day, as I walked along the shore on a windy night, feeling very depressed, I spotted tiny boats coming onto shore. They were offloading some supplies, some potatoes, and flour. They took them to little shops where the owners could make some muffins to sell. I had heard about the Marche Noir (Black Market), although I could not find where these "markets" were, except that it was perhaps the only food staples that I was actually finding. If they were caught, they could get 22 years in prison and huge fines, or just be shot where they stood. All food supplies were supposed to go through the central market under the surveillance of the Germans. A few days later, I saw one of the men of the Marche Noir being searched in the street after having disposed of a million boxes of sardines and boatloads of chocolate. Hearing about boatloads of chocolate, chocolate that I had so taken for granted. I fondly remember sitting in a café in Paris a decade ago, having a steaming cup of hot chocolate and a fluffy brioche. In my mind, I could smell the warm bread and luncheon hors *d'oeuvres* with all types of smoked or canned fish as well as paté. Now all I could do was dream of such things unless I could find some black-market food to buy. I would give most of what I had to Bobby, and he would give something to Mitzie. I was getting weaker and could barely ride the bike or climb the stairs.

My only friend left in all of Paris was Mme Cranovitz. She came to visit me one day, and seeing the state that we were in, she just took charge. She scurried about, cleaned up the mess Bobby made, caring for himself and Mitzi. Then she found an egg and some powdered milk, which she insisted that I share with Bobby.

(He gave a scrap to Mitzi.) I had been too ill the last few months to prepare anything. An area doctor said that my sickness was largely due to undernourishment and had given me a special letter signed by the commissariat, which enabled me to obtain powdered milk if we could find any. What good were the ration cards if there was nothing to buy? If meat were in the market, you could have 3 servings a week, but there was hardly ever any for one meal a week. One day, a French truck driver was passing by, and I asked him where he was going. He told me the name of the grocery store, and I ran to get there. As soon as he got there, he unloaded bushels of potatoes, and I was able to buy one small basket.

Everything at our apartment had to be locked up. Thieves would break into apartments and steal whatever food they could find. Since I was in a big, empty building, thieves always seemed to be rummaging through the building, not even realizing that we were there. As I headed out for food during the day, Bobby was alone with Mitzi. Fortunately, Mitzi would start to bark if someone came near the door.

I was also getting just too weak to carry any groceries up 5 flights of steps. I realized that there was another house down the road that was empty, where we could go without too much difficulty. We moved everything with a hand cart and left much behind. The house was near a place where they kept machines and airplane testing equipment. It was separated from the house by a strip of woods but was on what was called the route of thieves (route des voleurs). We kept hearing the bombardment of planes flying overhead all night long. The house had an old-fashioned garden door, difficult to enter. You then crossed the garden to a stairway door and finally up two flights to our door, which was double locked. It seemed safe, certainly safer than where we were. I had all my papers and notes for articles, as well as the tins of food that I had accumulated to have when no fresh food could be found. Madame Lizbet Cranovitz had stayed with us quite a bit now, helping to take care of us. She kept telling us how we would all be fine after the war. She had $200,000 worth of Russian stocks, which she was sure would be worth a fortune after the war. She also had expensive antique jewelry, which she said we could try to sell if we really needed money. The landlord of the new house took me outside one day to the garden, and I saw a beautiful sight. A garden full of cabbages. She had planted them the year before to feed the rabbits, but now had them for themselves and offered me a head. This was what our lives were reduced to: begging for a head of cabbage. I thought of Tolstoi, "The ground on which I stood was crumbling, there was nothing for me to stand on, that what I had been living for was nothing, that I had no reason for living." Then I thought of Bobby amidst the bombardments. The noise all night long was so bad that I couldn't sleep at night and took naps during the day. One day, while lying alone in my bedroom, I heard footsteps. I knew that Bobby was with a friend, so I called out to Lizbet and then heard the footsteps retreating. Later, we found that they had entered with a pass key and stolen several things. My best gloves, stockings, and some cans of food. We lived in constant fear of bombs, Germans, local thieves, and starvation. I hardly knew which was the worst.

Just at the point when all we had left was some oatmeal and a few unknown cans, I came across a shop selling bread and white butter made from whale oil that had come from Poland via the Germans. Finally, with my invalid cards from the doctor, I received a pint of milk a day that I shared with my son. All Fall and Winter, French women wore their snowsuits in their homes and on the Champs-Élysées. There was no heat anywhere.

One day, Madame Cranovitz declared very calmly, "I have used up everything that you have right now. Your friends have all explained that I now must kill you and serve you to Bobby and Mitzi!!" I looked at her. She sat down and explained, "I have been to six markets in this town and three villages around here in the last three days. At times, there is not one thing to be had. Not one vegetable, not one scrap of meat or fish." All she had found in Paris were some grapes. All we had was some bread and our cans of cassolettes, which I had hoped would last until we could find a way to leave. There was no macaroni, potatoes, or oil. When I could walk or ride my bicycle looking for food, I would quietly meet people who were on the same journey.

I also knew that I could not travel in my weakened state with a rambunctious, impetuous boy and a dog on a leash, as well as our belongings. I was totally depressed, and some days would just stay in bed. I felt like I could take no more. So, during these anxious weeks, my melancholy took over, and I just gave away Mitzie. I just could not feed him, and he just whimpered all day long. The pup that had charmed a ship and followed Bobby everywhere, I just gave away. I hoped that he would have a good home and food to eat. I couldn't think of any other alternative. Bobby cried and cried and would barely talk to me for weeks on end. He swore that he would never forgive me, but I couldn't listen to the poor dog whining from hunger. Could I ever forgive myself as I tried to hide my tears from Bobby? We loved that dog so much, now what would become of him? What would become of us?

Chapter 8
The Pendant

I was determined now that we would make it out of Meudon. I spoke to people on the street, anyone who was like me wandering looking for food, or huddling in doorways to stay out of the cold. You quietly met people. One person introduced you to another in passing or told you where to go for food. One old lady who had a liaison with a farmer smuggled us a pound of butter once a week for about a month. It was such a luxury, and we would slather it onto a thin slice of homemade bread. I would feel bad that my eating this was taking it away from some French child, but I knew that I had to get better if we were ever to leave Meudon, and get home to America. I had gotten rid of poor Mitzie and had come to realize that no Prince was coming to rescue us, no one to slay the dragons of hunger and fear. Only I could save us. Only I could slay the dragon and rise above it all.

One day, I bumped into a very nice older Polish man, who was a former soldier. We started speaking and we quickly realized that he also had to get away. We decided that we could help each other. It would be better for him as well if we travelled as a family. At first, he said that he had a car and would drive us. But then we decided that it was much too dangerous to drive. We decided that we would all dress as French peasants and leave the area on a wagon. Our hands were much to clean so we rubbed mud into the crevices, and the cuticles and put them under the nails. I had to look like a poor laborer that no one would care about. Bobby and I already looked malnourished, so we already looked gaunt and emaciated. I put on a black coat that I got from a neighbor who was larger than me, and then put a handkerchief on my head, brown makeup scuffed up my face and sunken cheeks. I also scuffed up Bobby's face and put on the rattiest clothes that he had. He told me to wear work gloves and drive the donkey because my hands would give me away. They were still too refined. My new Polish friend told me to be sure to always look down and don't look at them squarely. Our clothes and things were done up in big bundles on the back of the cart. With flowers, a bird cage, a clock, and hay covering the back of the wagon, Bobby was mostly hidden under it all. We rode the two-wheeled wagon and old donkey right past the German soldiers and they didn't even bother to stop us. We just kept riding without speaking and made it pretty far into the night. We finally stopped to decide what to do next. There were no passenger trains yet, nor would there be for weeks, maybe months. We would try to catch a freight train going in the right direction and pay the engineer something for letting us ride on the train. When the large sliding door of the freight car opened, we realized that there were some other men hidden in the straw on the train. Stowed away in the depths of the freight car, we rattled on toward Bordeaux, away from Meudon and Paris. One man on the train from Amiens told us that many engineers had been sent there to rebuild the parts of the city that had been bombed so that families living in the streets and alleyways could get back into their houses. The men had gone there to restore the water and sewage lines, but could not stay long because there was no food for the workmen.

We left the freight door open a little bit for fresh air as we moved on and I cried silent tears as we travelled by train across the French countryside. I remembered the beauty of the countryside where I had been just a decade earlier. When Johnny and I had gone to France before we had decided to journey outside of Paris and travel around. Our first stop was Mont. St. Michel, about 4 hours outside of Paris. When we told people that we planned to go to Mont. St. Michel back then, we were told to be sure to have one of Mme Poulard's omelets. They were celebrated as the best in the world. Every French person that we spoke to before our trip said, "Oh! If you go to Mont. St. Michel, you must be sure to eat one of Mme Poulard's omelets." It seemed that she had earned her reputation in a place where she flipped 20 eggs at a time. And of course, the wonderful taste of the final product. When we got off the train we came across a little hotel. We went through the gate and the woman told us that she would give us a beautiful room overlooking the sea. I took the card, and it said Hotel de la Confiance. Proprietor Mme Poulard. "Oh," I said, "so, you are Mme Poulard?" "Oui," she responded quietly. I have often heard about your omelets. She grunted and I took it as her being modest but then we found 4 other places that said Mme Poulard. I realized that it seemed that everyone was Mme Polard in Mont. St. Michel. Which was the true Mme Poulard omelette? We tried several, not being sure which was the famous one. I thought about how I could do a whole article about the variations on these omelets. I had often tried to write recipes of the many variations. We were headed in the direction of Mt. St. Michel and I thought of how just one egg, one egg any style would be so wonderful right now.

Johnny and I had gone to Barbizon next, a former artist's colony. Millet, Rousseau, Corot, and many others lived and worked there. It was very picturesque but then became too commercial because of its artistic fame. We had travelled through the emerald green forests to Fountainbleau. The trees were covered with velvety moss so that even your voice seemed muffled. I understood why all the artists wanted to paint there. How does emerald green now turn to a muddy brownish grey? As Bobby and I rumbled on the freight train through this same French countryside, there was no green anywhere. There was no longer even a glimpse of a cow or lamb or sheep. The fields were scorched. It was desolate. Even the trees seemed to have died. The fields had turned to hay.

Strasburg was the next town that Johnny and I were just crazy about. I told Bobby the story of the trip as we sat on the floor of the freight car. I explained how it had the loveliest cathedral, the cutest houses, and the funniest roofs you've ever seen because the roofs make such good nesting places, the town was just full of birds. The day we arrived was hot, so his dad and I rented bicycles, and we stayed in a lovely little mountain town on Lake Girard. On the next morning, we took a tram up the mountainside to the highest point. From that point, we could see the bald-faced mountain where Johnny had been in the trenches during World War I. The ride up was glorious, but the only trouble was that the bicycle kept falling off the tram car, causing a commotion. We finally reached the top and had lunch in one of the hotels which sat perched above the hill, commanding a view of the universe. After lunch, we started down on the bicycles, fortunately, the brakes held out and we coasted 30 km, about 20 miles. We stopped once when I needed a break. Strasburg with its quaint houses and streets was just as wide as the narrow footbridge leading over a canal. It was such a beautiful coast, such an adorable quaint little town. Peasants were making hay but it was the sleepiest looking countryside town. We followed the canal until we found Saint Nicholas for Hotel Beaurivage. It was a funny little old house like all the others with flower boxes looking at the canal. One of the most attractive things about these old places was that they were colored. Ours was pink. Many were a soft yellow, which is beautiful with the old shutters and brown timbers. These timbers were usually carved within an inch of their lives, and carefully painted but, of course, the paint was faded and peeling off, even then. At that time, it just gave them a sense of time. Beneath the age of the house was its inner beauty in its design. It must have been lovely when the whole town was decked out that way. It was a very old part of the town, just three blocks from the cathedral. One roof was as tall as the house with six or seven rows of little windows. The old market building on the corner street had a marble-shaped roof, sort of like a zigzag or a stepped pyramid from the front with roofs on the side. But now all the houses that we saw were in total disrepair. The roads were empty, deserted. Had everyone left France or were they just huddled in their homes without food or heat as we were in Meudon?

Johnny and I had travelled to Bordeaux, the same path we now took but on a passenger train. We then went on from there to Rome, ending up in Florence. We went to Milan, Budapest, to

Switzerland. I had decided right then that I would get a degree at the Sorbonne and would spend my life writing and travelling Europe. And now I was back, but in a Europe that was unrecognizable.

Rattling along in a cattle car of the freight train with Bobby, in late January, we were so cold and hungry. As I thought about this, I realized that we had been hungry since late June. I had dreamed of showing my son Europe and now all we saw was desolation. First, there had been those empty days, when Paris and the surrounding towns were in fear. So, I never did get to show him much of France and now that we were seeing more of the countryside, all that was seen was desperate desolation.

Suddenly, the train stopped, and the men opened the doors and leaned out. The train had reached a little junction town and there was loud talk and a lot of commotion from a few of the natives. It seemed that a bombardment was feared. There was the sound of strong motors, whirring planes. Then terrific explosions. They told us that they must wait and see if they can continue. We all sat there for hours in absolute silence and darkness. Even a baby that was with us never cried; he also sensed the oppressive fear in the air. We held our breath and clutched hands. After seemingly endless hours the train began to slowly trudge on to Bordeaux. At Bordeaux, the Polish officer left us to head towards

Spain. We stayed on the train to go to Arcachon to rest and recover so that I could make the journey the rest of the way home because we heard there was more food in Arachon; all the farms were in that area. Arachon was a seaside town near Bordeaux and there were very few German soldiers there, so we were told.

We found a quaint little hotel. The woman who ran the hotel sat by the counter with her head in her hands. Her face was gaunt and tear-stained. She blurted out to us, "Do you know Pierre, my husband?" she had no news of her husband for a month. She didn't know if he had been killed or was in a German prison. She was so glad to have someone to talk to, someone who would just listen to her. We shared stories of our experiences. She told us that reports said that the provisions for Paris were "splendid" and that cities in occupied France were well supplied. The German propaganda machine told people that their town was the only one in short supply. I told anyone who would listen at all, that they were completely misinformed about the situation in Paris. I recalled pears for 10 francs[19] and it was so rare that in expensive shops they were wrapped with cotton and ribbons. I told them how I had seen empty stalls at the largest market in Rue Saint Lazare. In Montmartre, I had seen even the horse meat markets

---

[19] 10 francs was equal to 20 cents in 1940. In purchasing power today that is the equivalent of approximately 4 dollars for a single pear!

and fish markets shutter their doors and windows because they could get no supplies. There was no rest, no way to stop the anxiety, the nervousness, the insipid fear. After a few days of rest and some food, we travelled to Bourdeaux to be ready to sail on the first ship to America.

We arrived in Bourdeaux, just missing the bombardments of the train tracks. If we had waited just a few days more we would not have made it into Bourdeaux. The bombings had taken out all of the tracks that we had just travelled on. We carefully chose lodging on a back street away from the docks. The very first night in Bourdeaux I heard the landlord rapping on the doors telling us to get out quickly. "Don't waste any time about it." When he heard Bobby's excited voice, he grabbed his hand and with his big flashlight he led us to a big damp basement of a neighboring house. It was actually good to sit down on the whitewashed walls with others. A grandmother sat in a rocking chair that she left down there. Old men were telling war stories from previous wars. Each time when the bombers came at night we slipped our winter coats over our pajamas and went back to the huge basement in the building a few doors down.

We spent Christmas and New Year's Eve in this way. We sat in the basement night after night listening to the far-off bombardments terrified that they would come closer. We heard on the radio that a factory had been bombed and about the wreckage of more train lines. The radio rasped out information that three Italian destroyers at Bourdeaux were completely wrecked. Trying to drown out the news on the radio, Bobby and I reminisced about Christmases past. We both agreed that the best one was the one just a couple of years before with Molly Brown.

I told the people in the basement the story. On the day before Christmas, I had been strolling down Fifth Avenue with boxes of Christmas cookies for people that I knew in Manhattan. Tucked under my arm was my manuscript, Alive in Wonderland, which I hoped to show to an editor. I had written asking for an appointment but hadn't heard. Just as I was on my way to the publishers. I suddenly bumped into Mrs. JJ (Leadville Johnny) Brown, better known as the Unsinkable Molly Brown (although her name is actually Margaret). Perhaps, you've heard about her.

Margaret Tolbin who became my duchess, Molly Brown was born in a small town in Hannibal Missouri by the Mississippi River to recent Irish Catholic immigrants. They were progressive and encouraged education and equality. At 13, she was already working in a factory laboring long hours for low pay. She and her brother decided to go west and Margaret landed in Leadville Colorado where she worked, but also helped out in soup kitchens and with other charities. Here she met JJ Brown a respectable mining engineer who was a primary shareholder in the Little Johnny gold mine. They were dirt poor like everyone else, until suddenly, unbelievably, and in a flash, in 1893, they discovered gold in the Little Johnny mine and became millionaires. They moved to Denver and bought what would become a magnificent home. Because Molly had seen and lived in poverty, and slums and seen homelessness as well as starving children she became involved with the Progressive reformers and pushed for public baths, more parks, and city improvements. With their new wealth, they travelled extensively going to Russia, India, Italy, and France. Margaret wrote articles about their travels and even published a cookbook. She became my mentor in many ways.

The town was then named after him as his mine proved to produce a lot of gold and silver. But JJ died soon after and in 1922, Molly was left on her own. She, with another partner's widow, took over the Little Johnny mine. She showed the world that women were just as intelligent and capable. She fought against "not being a man" and that women could do anything. She was a role model for so many women. She had become very rich, very lavish, and very original in every way! She dressed eccentrically and that threw lots of people off. She insisted on being her person and doing as she pleased, no matter what anyone, including her children, said to her.

Her wealth and popularity earned her the nickname "the Duchess." She became a member of the National Woman's Party, and she rallied President Calvin Coolidge in Rapid City, S. D., to seek his support for the equal rights amendment to the federal constitution. She often took her special guest with her, Princess Stephanie Dalforouki, "a member of the former reigning house of Russia, and an exile from her home, who, poor and unfriended, had found shelter in the heart and home of Mrs. Brown."[20] Molly Brown would even run as a candidate of Progressives and Democrats. She ran for office in Colorado when women were not considered fit for office. She stated, "There seems to be a general feeling that in all the States where women vote, there should be a certain number of women office-holders. And because I've been fortunate enough to live a broad life and to know many sorts and conditions of people, my friends tell me that I am well-fitted to represent the State of Colorado at Washington.[21]" She defined herself as a suffragette, played baseball with her brothers, rode horses, and even played Polo, she was interested in sports and meanwhile also raised 2 children.

The Duchess later traveled all over the world once her Johnny was gone. Her wealth enabled her to be with all of the Dukes,

---

[20] Molly Brown museum clippings
[21] Molly Brown museum clippings

Duchesses, and royalty of Europe. But her real fame came when she travelled on the ill-fated ship the Titanic. She is best known for not only being a survivor of the Titanic but for getting out in a lifeboat with 18 others, taking an oar herself, and insisting that they go back to look for other survivors. She told them all not to fear if they stayed with her because she was a survivor and was the "Unsinkable Molly Brown." After that, she became known forever as the "Unsinkable Molly Brown." Her fame as the *Titanic* survivor helped her to further promote the rights of workers and women, education and literacy for children, and historic preservation. During World War I in France, she worked with the <u>American Committee for Devastated France</u> to rebuild areas behind the front line and helped wounded soldiers. She was awarded the French <u>*Légion d'Honneur*</u> for her good citizenship, activism, and philanthropy in America.

I had first met her in Paris a decade ago, when the editor from the *International Herald Tribune*, or maybe it was UPI, sent me off to interview with her. My boss in Paris had warned me that she was "terrible," and that she would probably, if she liked me, shower me with awful presents, once she had given him for Easter a chick with lots of little chicks. He said she didn't know what to do with all of her money. You could imagine with what distaste I approached the Duchess Brown, Leadville Johnny's widow. She approached me with distaste, as well. I don't know what she'd heard. Anyway, she seemed disgusted with the whole UPI. In all the time I was in Paris interviewing her from time to time and writing up my pieces, she never once gave me any presents. She only sent medicine to my boss, which he sadly needed but never took. When I left to go back to the United States with Johnny, she also returned to the United States for the first time in years. I supposed that she had gone to Denver Colorado, where her main home was, and I didn't ever expect to see her again. My two nicest write-ups of her were published after she left. (She later told me that one of them was resold by the UPI to the association of hotel owners for their magazine).

When I bumped into her in NYC a few years later on Fifth Avenue, she was all dressed up in one of her numerous disguises. She had hairpins all over her head. It was raining and my hair was just dripping, so she gave me a whole bunch of hairpins to put up my hair. She pulled out her longest gold hairpin and helped me put it in and gave it to me. She then suddenly asked if I had been to the Waldorf. "We must go for tea," she said although it was lunchtime. I had been wanting to go but couldn't afford it so I was so delighted when she suggested that we go. Imagine my delight that the duchess should mention taking me to the Waldorf. But we didn't end up at the Waldorf. That wouldn't make a good story.

Instead, she took me to the Ambassador, on Park Avenue where she said Merry Christmas, Merry Christmas, Merry Christmas to everyone, to all the managers, sub managers, etc. She shouted Merry Christmas joyfully back and came running over to me. She asked me what I'd been doing, and I told her and she said that only that morning she received a letter from her sister in Beverly Hills telling of a woman influential in publishing in New York. She decided to take me there right after lunch. We had tea, and a baked potato, at the Ambassador in the most charming surroundings, autumn ferns everywhere and an orchestra playing heavenly music. Mrs. Brown was in fine fettle and told such funny stories that I nearly died of laughter. She then preached a gospel sermon and I was enchanted. Afterward, she took me to deliver my two remaining packages of cookies and go to this publishing woman's office. She began to take taxis every place just to go one block – and I couldn't bear it so I told her I couldn't and convinced her to climb onto the top of the Fifth Avenue buses with me. She is such a real Duchess – but such a good sport. We did a preliminary farewell and started home as she kept saying, "I'm surfeited with civilization I'm surfeited with civilization I am surfeited with civilization." So, of course, I took my cue that she wanted something more simple and less excessive, so I asked her out to my new place in Connecticut for Christmas dinner. I thought that it was only a courtesy to invite her to our home for

Christmas.   Johnny's brother was coming, but my relatives couldn't, and I thought it would be lovely to have an old friend from Paris. Besides, she's been introducing me as Miss Smith all day for no reason at all, except that she couldn't remember Moody so I felt that she might almost be one of the family. She said she had three invitations already - Helen Astor asked her, and I don't know who else but she would consider it.

So imagine how shocked I was when a car pulled up to our little house and this woman stepped out of the taxi all decked out like Mrs. Santa Claus. She wore a red velvet suit with a *breitswanz*, a German fur, and matching with a muff and scarf. She even wore a little *pelerine*, a small cape that covered her shoulders. Only she could have a red velvet and fur suit, such a Duchess!

We had a marvelous time the whole afternoon while she was there. And the things she brought me! I had mentioned that I was going to try to go to Philadelphia with my novel and some other things, so she brought me a traveling case, two books as if I had some time to read, a handkerchief with marvelous lace, and a string of green beads like some of her own which I had admired. Bobby was an angel the whole day and everybody thought him so pretty and good. He got loads of presents – some galoshes and a sweater, some blankets, and some toys, he even got a lovely big velvet cat from Uncle Bob and Blanca.

The Duchess told us such great stories, like how she used to knit green ties for Thomas Lipton (the creator of Lipton tea). Lipton raced his yacht called the *Shamrock* five times unsuccessfully for the America's Cup between 1899 and 1930. Hailed as "the best of all losers," he was awarded a special cup for his repeated failures, and the publicity of his attempts helped his tea gain popularity in the States. Mrs Brown sent him a real Colorado shamrock before the last race. It was she who really started the movement which got him finally into the royal society before his death. My poor family didn't quite understand her, but Bobby and I had a marvelous time. At our little modest home in Connecticut, the Duchess recited poetry to us all day and yodeled to Bobby. I liked her so well. She had been 3 times around the world and still couldn't read a timetable or understand maps. The Duchess was an extravagant but real person.

At the end of the evening, we hugged and then called her a cab when she suddenly announced that the worldly, Duchess Molly Brown had no money to get home. She gave a porter $10 thinking it was a dollar bill when she came and asked him for a quarter back. She had to borrow money to get out to us and borrow more to get back. There she is with $40 million or so and she had to borrow money to get back into the city, though isn't that like her?

As I got to know her in Paris and then became re-acquainted in NYC she really was my hero. She didn't care what anyone thought and believed that she was equal to any man. She wrote articles, travelled, raised two children, and stayed her own person. We stayed in touch over the next year, writing letters and visiting her at the Barbizon Hotel where she stayed with other progressive women.

The Barbizon Hotel is a story in itself. The Barbizon hotel was a "23-story edifice of coral-pink brick and sandstone façade with Romanesque, Gothic, and Moorish embellishment. It housed 700 guest rooms, just big enough for a single bed and a petite easy chair, and had the then-impressive technology of a radio built into the wall. Most rooms shared hallway bathrooms, dormitory-style. There was a library, a pool and a gym, a roof garden, and studios to practice painting or singing arias. Discreet entrances off the lobby led to a coffee shop, a bookstore, and a few other shops that were all for the well-heeled and well-bred woman. A mezzanine over the lobby allowed women to scope out the dates coming to pick them up. At afternoon tea, a lady played a pipe organ.[22]" As women had gained some new independence, hotels for single upscale women began to appear. The concept was that a single

---

[22] Maria Ricapito, "Inside the Barbizon Hotel for Women", *Marie Claire* Apr 6, 2021

woman in NYC was akin to being stranded on a deserted island."[23]

Women had shredded the shackles of Victorian dress and the New Modern Woman, "was sleek, more simplified and dignified and yet still feminine. The Barbizon was the definition of the New Woman. The outside looked bold and masculine but inside, where men were not allowed to go, it was feminine and more delicate, with a modern French style. Molly Brown was delighted that each room was tastefully designed and furnished with a radio built in.

It was perfect for a woman like Molly Brown who never seemed to like to stay in one place for very long. She had her house in Newport, loved to be in Paris, and of course, had her large home in Denver. When in NYC she could be in the solarium, engage in conversation with young talented, and bright women and the city itself was at her feet where she could dine and go to plays and meet other socialites. The inside lobby where guests could be entertained was filled with large windows and potted plants throughout the two-story high space. The mezzanine led to an oak-paneled library. Named after the Barbizon art movement the colors were reflective of the art of its namesake. The namesake was to encourage women who were creative while the space was to

---

[23] Barbizon hotel page 25

make them think that they were in the town of Barbizon outside of Paris. Articles were written about the new American woman. The National Association of Junior Leagues was on the 22nd floor of the Barbizon and the space was featured in Vogue. All this added to the lure of the Barbizon for Modern women of all ages and types. As it became better known while still being built it was advertised for the artistic "but rarefied young lady, for the respectable but modern woman.[24]"

Molly Brown preferred the artist area of the hotel with the high ceilings and light streaming in. The new post-suffragette mentality demanded that the mind and body be nourished.

Having been an avid advocate for the suffragette movement, she found the flappers annoying and gaudy, and that they drank too much. It was Prohibition when Molly Brown moved into the Barbizon and bars in the area attracted many of the women from the hotel. The flappers were not the New Woman that Molly Brown had envisioned. Rather Sue Moody White was. Molly Brown saw me as someone who was, like her, from out west but was sophisticated and had lived in Paris. I tried to be stylish and certainly enjoyed new gourmet food and elegant dress. I was a mother and worked and wrote, exactly the kind of woman that

---

[24] Barbizon Hotel, p. 41

Molly Brown wanted to help and promote as the new woman. She became my mentor in many ways.

I cherished the letters that we wrote to each other. Our letters were about politics, poetry, food, recipes, and children. She would often include clippings about various subjects to me.

She had come back from Paris in 1931 and what many people did not realize was that she no longer had the fortune that she once had. I soon learned that she needed a place that was respectful and yet not too expensive. At the Barbizon, she had a room of her own, and yet was surrounded by music, art, and theater, from a roster of residents in the arts. Her soundproof room allowed her to take voice lessons and she could converse with people in the arts in the library, lounge, dining room, or even in the elevator.

She had complained to me of fierce migraines and would rest in her room for days but when I told her to see her doctor, she would tell me that she was as vibrant as ever. I was devastated when I learnt that she died in her sleep on October 26, 1932, at the Barbizon Hotel. It was later told that she had a brain tumor. I knew that I could be independent and on my own if I needed to be. I wanted to be the New Woman that my Dutchess admired.

The next Christmas in NYC was certainly not as exciting with the Duchess no longer around. The economic depression had gotten worse, but nothing was as horrible as this Christmas in Bourdeaux, huddled in a basement with strangers. We ate the last two Nuremberg cookies that I had saved from the early days of the bombardments for our Christmas meal.

Despite the adversities, it was nice to be in the South of France where it was warmer, more open and the sun was shining compared to shivering in the unheated Meudon apartment. I walked out into the sunshine, determined to find the American Consulate. I walked past the Bourse a large, beautiful square, and found it filled with German soldiers. The square was one of the most recognizable sites in Bourdeaux. It had been built in 1730-1775 along the Garonne River. In 1869, a large fountain surrounded by sculptures of the three graces was installed. I decided to leave and come back another day when the soldiers might be gone. But when I returned the majestic beautiful square had been destroyed. It was all gone. Completely demolished. It lay there in ruins. There was nothing left of the beautiful gingerbread houses. Only a few ribs of the house frames lay smoldering like decayed bones of a skeleton surrounding what was left of the large fountain. There had been a horrific bombardment lasting from 8 PM to 2 AM and we could hear it from our room throughout the night but couldn't tell where it was coming from. "They came in continuous waves," a man on the trolley told me. I walked along the docks where factories and storehouses had been hit and only saw twisted steel. Cafes and bars were now gone. Private homes near the docks also lay in ruin.

I could only tell Bobby about what it once was like. To stroll down the boulevard as the smells of fresh bread, grilled meat, and cheeses pour out from the shops. Bobby just kept saying to find a little restaurant where we could just have one proper meal. He was right, we just wanted one real French meal, as I remembered strolling in Paris, Bordeaux, or NYC, going for a walk in the early twilight. On side streets, windows cast long shadows. Suddenly confronted by a sign that just says "The Inn." It hung over the street from a small cottage whose small windows had tie-back curtains, and small green wreaths as if from a page out of Dickens, with an array of antique, faded heirloom plates. What went into fixing up a restaurant? How did the colors and images get across the tone of the place? It was more than just the food; it was also the ambience that could transform the visitor to another time or a far-off place. The decoration and the unique smells transported you to a little café in Paris or Moscow. I had written many articles about various restaurants in NYC, Paris, or Rome before, and this little restaurant reminded me of my travels and the people that I met in Europe, of a happier, easier time. But you couldn't eat memories, and there was little to actually eat at this Inn.

I finally made it to the American consulate office in Bordeaux. I was able to get some letters that had been forwarded to the embassy. They also forwarded letters from those still in Paris, as well as monies owed to me from the newspaper that was thankfully still paying me, although I had not written much. I had written a couple of articles about starvation, and now had an open post office to send them to. There was a letter from my old landlord from the big building in Meudon. In the letters from America, they seemed to have no idea about the severity of the famine. They all thought it was temporary. But I had already been through it for nine months. How much more could we endure? There were a few letters from my husband Johnny from months ago, and one more recent one. None of the promised money was included. I hesitated to open them.

We finally found another place to stay, a pension, run by a woman whose brother owned a farm. We now occasionally had an omelet and vegetables and we thought that we had finally landed someplace safe and with food. We were so very excited that I had some money to pay for this. Once a week, we had a bite of chicken or rabbit. It was the most that we had eaten in months. We thought that we would now be fine until we could go to America. But our joy was short-lived. A few days later, the owner of the Inn announced that her brother would no longer be bringing food from Brittany. He had no more rabbits or chickens or gas to even truck the vegetables. We had no idea how long it would be until we could get on a ship for America, how we would survive until then, or what our life would be like when we returned.

Chapter 9
Gold Chain

We were advised that the Red Cross would help to take us home but in the interim there was a group of Quakers that could help us. I met up with them and told them that my mother was Quaker. They immediately took me and Bobby to another location, a place where they were helping refugee children. When Panzers had rolled into France the American Quakers, who happened to be in France, began to immediately supply relief to as many as they could with their small resources in the districts where they happened to be. They provided babies with milk. Now, the Quakers' noon meal of rice and cocoa that they provided was all that some received each day. They all worked under the little flag or armband of the Quaker star, symbol of the Friends War Victims Relief Committee. This group was first formed in 1870 to relieve civilian sufferers of the Franco Prussian War in Northeastern France. Other Americans stranded in France began to join the Quakers. I was so proud to have come from a Quaker family and regretted that I had dismissed them and their beliefs every time my mother tried to inculcate me in their traditions.

One woman that I met there was Caroline Hill. For 10 days, she struggled to travel from Marseilles to Bordeaux in her car, trying to save three young French girls. She used whatever money she had to hide from bombardments and machine gun attacks on the highway. On the first night, fifteen miles outside of Paris, her car broke down. She found a truck and then a tractor to pull them. Finally, a young boy, whom they met along the way in a little town was able to fix the car. They slept in a farmyard one night with 100 employees who were evacuated from a large Normandy farm. They had to keep finding places to stay and often had to run into the woods to hide in ditches. Another night, they slept in an old, deserted cheese factory. Caroline would stay up all night to protect the girls. Often, all they had to eat all day was one raw egg. They finally reached Bordeaux in a state of physical collapse, tongues parched from the inability to find clean water, and memories of food something in a distant past.

Caroline Hill was one of many now trying to help others. The Quakers wanted to do more, but there was little to no food to be found, even for sale. Foodstuffs might be secured from other countries, but then you have to find the proper currency needed to purchase them. After that, they had to get permission from the government of that country to export the food to France. Finally, it was necessary to obtain licenses from Washington, DC to pay for each purchase. It was a heartbreaking amount of time, while needy children and mothers were crowding around the Quaker volunteers with hunger in their eyes. They also waited for shipments of vitamins, which were so badly needed, considering the malnourishment. The first shipment of vitamins that came, while I was there, was mixed with chocolate and was distributed in the form of small chocolate squares, each containing Vitamin A and paper wrappings bearing the inscription, "Gift of the American Quakers." More than half a million of these were given in Lyon alone. Later, when chocolate was scarce, it was given as a drop on a piece of bread. In another area, some Quakers found a group of 2,000 children stranded and starving in an area that was heavily bombed. All the children had been told to run into the woods while their town was bombed. The Quakers built a little village for themselves in the woods so that they were protected. The Quakers distributed tinned milk, sugar, rice, cod liver oil, and the vitamins as much as was feasible. Meanwhile, the local women tried to gather as much food as they could from the local farms. With the shortage of oil and gasoline, the farmers could not get their produce to the cities, and the Quakers would pay the farmers for something. What started as 10 or 12 Quakers, who just happened to be in France, developed into a staff of about 120 volunteers. They handled all the funds for French organizations in America as well as for the Red Cross. I was happy to help and felt like I was finally doing something for others. I wrote an article and got it out to be published so that Americans might read about what was going on. My pen could have power. The article was first published in a Quaker paper but was soon picked up by other publications.

My time with the Quakers reminded me of my heritage and what was the strength of my character. I might not be able to fight with a gun, but I could do as my grandfather had for the Civil War and with the abolitionists. My heritage was not only of the Quakers but also of what came to be called "Bleeding Kansas," and a grandfather fighting the Quantrill brothers. I had a place in the fight for equality, justice, and human rights.

I had heard stories about my grandfather since I was little, or when sitting on his lap. But I never paid much attention. He was just grandpa. But when my father died, I had gone home, just a few years earlier, to sort out his affairs. There I found boxes of papers, manuscripts, books, journals, and letters that belonged to my grandfather. I asked a lot of questions to my mother and my aunt about him. I did research into who he really was. As I read his letters, journals, and books, I began to realize that Lawrence, Kansas, my birthplace, had a history of abolitionist and suffragette activism of which my family was a part.

I grew up in Lawrence, known for its fields of sunflowers, which have always towered over picket fences, dotting the broad expanses of the plains with their bright yellow flowers and the deep purple hollyhocks. Oat and corn grew tall and hid the goats and chickens, and horses from the outside world in the many small farms. One would think of Lawrence, Kansas, as a peaceful place, a refuge, on the surface, but the reality is that abolitionists, suffragettes, and Quakers journeyed from Vermont, Indiana, and Texas to what they hoped would be the 34th state and a free anti-slavery state in the mid-19th century.

My hometown of Lawrence, Kansas, was founded in 1854 by the New England Emigrant Aid Society to keep the territory free from slavery. With the belief that the U.S. should expand its reach, the Kansas-Nebraska Act was established in 1854, opening the Kansas and Nebraska territories for settlement. Voters could determine whether the new states were free or not. It was said that Lawrence was one of the few cities in the U.S. founded strictly for political reasons. The large area of the Kansas Territory extended west to the Rocky Mountains. With the opportunity to influence the state's future, abolitionists and Quakers moved to the territory, prepared to fight for a cause. Immigrant aid societies sponsored settlement from the Northeast, which supported the free-state movement. Southerners, particularly from Missouri, crossed the border to vote for slavery. The famous abolitionist, John Brown, and his sons came to the territory to fight proslavery forces until he was hanged in 1859. Joel Moody, my grandfather, took up the fight by joining the military. Lawrence, Kansas, would come to be called "Bleeding Kansas." After drafting four constitutions, Kansas eventually entered the Union as a free state on January 29, 1861, forming a state government based largely on the federal government and other state models. President Abraham Lincoln signed the Homestead Act in 1862, offering incentives to settle in the West.

The Civil War had reached what was then the Western border of the United States when Joel Moody, who had just finished college, joined the fight for Kansas. He served in the Civil War, starting as a private and was quickly promoted to lieutenant, finishing his military career as a captain in the Second Indian Regiment and commanding a company. He left behind political and philosophical essays as well as poetry to make sure that everyone remembered the struggles. He showed the power of the pen as he also began to write political essays and extensive poetry, including a history of Kansas in poetic verse.

He wrote a poem about John Brown[25]:

Then came John Brown close on his path,

slash and boldly passing to his den,

slash him struck an awful blow, and when

the shackles broke and fell from men

he rides in roared and demons wrath...

11 slaves are now set free

 a kindly stroke for those who fell

 adjust and righteous parallel

their freedom one and strange to tell

Kansas has gained her liberty.

The theme for the master sculptures hand,

slash his ancient glory and renowned

slash the waiting multitude shell crown,

will the remote appear, John Brown;

but it will be found in every land.

His glory heralded by Cedars,

in marble cut; by poet Sun;

and he's rude image shall be hung

---

25 All of Joel Moody's poems included in this book come directly from the book that
Joel Moody wrote, *The Song of Kansas and Other Poems*, Topeka Kansas: Geo E. Crane
1890

round the charm neck, and every tongue

shall praise him is the saint of years.

And here, in Kansas, we shall raise

the statue to the undying theme.

With sculptured art, we shall proclaim,

slash the fond memorial of his name,

which the shell stand and speak his praise.

Bright star of Kansas! Now thy place

is fixed: a bright central gem,

in Columbia is diadem;

which, like the star of Bethlehem,

points out a savior of the race

Quaker families began to enter the territory following the passage of the Kansas-Nebraska Act. The Quakers, including my Grandfather's family, were among the first group of white people to admonish slavery and ban any Quaker from ever owning slaves. In turn, they were very actively involved in the Underground Railroad. By the end of the year of 1857 about 200 had come to the new settlements in Kansas, including my family on my mother's side.

Several of the other new residents, such as Abolitionist Robert Gaston Elliot, set up newspapers, shared information, be it anti-slavery information, or about new settlements. The Lawrence of dirt streets and shanties was being transformed as companies moved in and graded the levee, fixed the streets, and opened pool halls and saloons, building new large-scale brick buildings. Even those pro-slavery residents were glad to see the improvements to their town, as it became increasingly prosperous and independent. The influx of people made Kansas City and Lawrence, Kansas, into real cities.

Joel Moody would later write of the issues facing Kansas at the time in his book of poetry called 'Song of Kansas' (Topeka: Geo. W Crane, 1890)

Slavery, like the great python
Apollo sluice; bread in the slime
of earth, whose birth was the first crime
against mankind, and the sublime
iniquity of hell to dethroned.

Of slavery is recognized
By the first law of man and God;
Kansas we own, and on her side
shall stand no man, unless he not slash to

> our great truth, and be baptized
>
> and taken into fellowship with all the dear beloved ones
>
> who are not classed with freedom son…
>
> The dogs of war! Let no church open
>
> the door to him who cannot pray
>
> slavery scores! Let no man stay
>
> on Kansas soil, who cast the race
>
> of heavenly light on seeking hope.

After drafting four constitutions, Kansas eventually entered the Union as a free state on January 29, 1861, forming a state government based largely on the federal government and other state models. President Abraham Lincoln signed the Homestead Act in 1862, offering incentives to settle in the West. But the Kansas-Missouri border was in reality a hotbed of tension and violence. And Lawrence, Kansas, would come to be called "Bleeding Kansas."

In the summer, when the town was covered with dust from the dried fields, bandits of guerrillas led by William Quantrill stormed into the Kansas territory from slave state Missouri to attack the known abolitionists. Quantrill's father was known to have beaten him and his 8 other brothers and sisters. In 1854, just as the Kansas-Nebraska Act was signed, William Quantrill's father died of tuberculosis and alcoholism, and his mother struggled to survive, turning their home into a boarding house and sending William out to work. Always a good student, William got a position as a teacher in a small school in Ohio and then at a lumberyard. But he had a fierce temper, and by the time he turned 17, he had killed a man. He travelled home with no more money than when he had left. Unhappy to live in a shack outside the boarding house, William, like many others, decided to travel to Kansas to get a plot of land. But he borrowed money, which he didn't pay back, and again was in trouble with the law. Angry and disheartened, he roamed the woods with his rifle, hunting for his dinner. He tried teaching in Lawrence for a while, but he drank, played poker, gambled, won, and then, of course, lost it all. He never seemed to be pro slavery until he figured out that he could make money capturing runaway slaves. Quantrill met up with other mostly former Confederate soldiers such as Cole Younger, William T. 'Bloody Bill' Anderson, and the James brothers. Emboldened by his association with a new group of outlaws, Quantrill and his men overcame a small Union outpost at Aubry, Kansas, and ransacked the town.

His reign of terror had begun.

On March 11, 1862, Quantrill joined Confederate forces under Colonel John T. Hughes and took part in an attack on

Independence, Missouri. After what became known as the First Battle of Independence, the Confederate government decided to secure the loyalty of Quantrill by issuing him a 'formal army commission' with the rank of Captain. On September 7, 1862, after midnight, Quantrill with 140 of his men captured Olathe, Kansas. There, he surprised 125 Union soldiers and forced them to surrender. On October 5, 1862, Quantrill attacked and destroyed Shawneetown, Kansas, and torched the rebuilt settlement. The Union army fought back, and in 1863, the Union commander organized groups of white and African American troops. Union military rounded up the wives and sisters of Quantril and his bandits and put them in a separate building to get Quantril and his men to come back for them. But on August 14, the building in Kansas City, Missouri, where the women were being held, collapsed, killing 5. Quantrill took out his revenge on Lawrence, Kansas.

Joel Moody was in the Union army at the time, and he later wrote in his book of poetry about Lawrence, Kansas that he remembered before Quantrill's bloody attack:

Why? Nestled in the lovely veil
We are now the Kansas gently Flo
serene and where the LILY grows

like drooping love beside the rose and with the powers of
peace prevail,

there, Laurence stands, a lovely queen
of May, sweet Lawrence, freedom's child
cradled in love and taught the mild
and gentle ways of truth, she smiled
in graceful beauty not unseen

The love of man from and she taught;
she taught that human rights are dear;
she loved the home and sought to cheer
sad hearts, and she erected here
a citadel for honest thought

But Quantrill had no regard for the Lawrence, Kansas, that
Joel Moody described. Quantril retaliated with a vengeance and
said that his motivation for the attack was "to plunder and destroy
the town in retaliation for Osceola." That was a reference to the
Union's attack on Osceola, Missouri, in September 1861, led by
Senator James H. Lane.

In the middle of the night on August 21, 1863, without
warning, Quantrill brought 450 men, including notorious outlaws
such as the Younger brothers and Jesse James, to Mount Oread in

Lawrence. Then, early in the morning, Quantrill descended from Mount Oread and attacked Lawrence. They kidnapped 10 farmers, forcing them to show the rowdy group the way into Lawrence, Kansas. They then summarily murdered them all. Awakened by the shooting, people screaming and horses running wild, other farmers ran out from their homes and were shot in the street. More homes were invaded, and houses were burnt to the ground with people still in their beds. Lawrence was in ashes. Only 3 stores were left standing. Robert Elliot, a journalist, left an account of Quantrill's raid on Lawrence, as told by R.G. (Robert Gaston) Elliott from his vantage point in the Eldridge House hotel.

"At the Eldridge House, the help were just entering upon their respective duties, and the guests were locked in slumber, when only those alert or most easily wakened heard a few desultory shots, fired at a distance, but in a minute followed by volleys much nearer. Then all at once bedlam broke loose, with whooping and yelling, a storm of promiscuous firing, and the clattering of a thousand hoofs on the hard-beaten streets as horsemen dashed through the town, many of them at a mad gait, firing at everyone they saw running and into every window of the hotel where a head was exposed."

[I] "… was taken prisoner with others in the Eldridge House where I boarded, put under guard, and after it had been fired, conducted to another house…After being ke[t this way for 4 hours. . . We broke free and ran, and being near the river bank, all who could get horses and arms organized and started to pursue the bandits."

The Quantrill gang had ridden into Lawrence and, in a few hours, killed 150 men and burned 185 buildings to the ground. They then rode as fast as possible back to Missouri with the Union cavalry behind them. Quantrill, then 27, was shot in the back while trying to escape. He later died in a military prison hospital in Louisville.

Joel Moody wrote:

"The ashes here of Lawrence, – there

the type of press, the drunken glee,

slash the dust from trail of trees and see;

here is the bullet shot at me,

slash and hear the slimy serpents glare. "

 And later he wrote…

Abolitionist, Soto said;

Annata meeting held today,

it was ruled that they cannot stay,

but before I would go away,

if then I would fight till I was dead.

With the struggles of the civil war at his doorstep, Joel Moody abandoned his planned law practice to join the state legislature and later became a state senator, and then Secretary of State, to influence the course of history in Kansas for African Americans and women. His books, articles, and poems were widely circulated.

Moody wrote

"Kansas, my pride! You never saw slash me fail!

And you shall have the rain.

You save me once upon the plane

from wolves and ones from being slain.

Joel Moody fought with his hands, his guns and his pen against slavery as well as the oppression of women.

As Quakers, they had insisted upon the spiritual equality of women and all men as well. Quaker women preached, published treatises, and traveled in a kind of itinerant ministry. The most famous abolitionist and suffragette who was a Quaker was Lucretia Mott, who helped to set up the Women's Rights Convention at Seneca Falls. Other Suffragette activists such as Clarina I H Nichols also migrated to Kansas under the auspices of the New England Emigrant Aid Company. She would campaign for the equal rights of women, believing that it was easier to effectuate new laws for women in a new state than to change the laws of New England states, where the laws were ingrained in the culture. The voice of freedom echoed in the press as the best way to get the word out. It was the power of the pen that echoed across Kansas. Her basic argument was that women should either be allowed to vote or be exempt from taxation. Her eloquent and logical analysis of the suffrage question caused the editor of the Topeka Tribune to remark that "the women of Kansas have in her a faithful, powerful yet unassuming champion, and they should stick by her, to use a familiar political expression, and not leave her to labor along without publicly expressed sympathy and support." The press was the only way that political opinions could be fully expressed, and people rallied together. Joel Moody brought these sentiments to my family even as I grew up. I grew up with the idea embroiled in my mind that the pen was mightier than the bayonet.

In Joel Moody's book, *The Science of Evil,* he wrote about the status of women and how Prostitution is, in fact, the man's fault because of the way women are treated in society. Prostitution arises because of men's lust and domination of women. Treating them as property only naturally arises that poor women see a need that they can fulfill because of the men's lust. It is the story of supply and demand. If the woman is already seen as no more than property. He wrote that, "…. She was compelled to be faithful; to lie at his feet; to acknowledge him as her lord and master; to submit to him as his slave."… "Husband and wife are one, and the husband is that one. If the woman no longer confers superiority, no longer worships her husband, then the marriage would only depend on tyranny and want… If women are equal, then marriages might be destroyed and prostitution might dissipate. Women would have their own equal property. Men would have to worship women as women worship men. … So long as a woman worships a man, that man can control her; he becomes in the strictest sense her lord and master." "In inferior races," he said, "this superiority of man acknowledged by women is her submission to being a slave. If the slave did not worship and give in to the master, then there could not be a slave. There must be the one who demands and the one who supplies." Riches and poverty are the poles of a cumulative force. Similarly, an excess of wealth creates an equal excess of poverty, "every prince of fortune is complemented by a squad of beggars…" "If you wished to kill a tree, you would be called insane…by cutting off here and there a small limb; for many more would spring out where you had cut off one… We must strike at the root of the problem at man more and not the woman…. He does not see that it is his tyranny." No, it is not the slave who must be killed to abolish slavery, nor the prostitute who must be harmed to destroy Prostitution. Perhaps the situation will not change in the right direction until women, the enslaved, and the victim, are taught to see their true condition. She must be educated. She must be wise to the affairs of church and state to realize the force of an idea. She must know science. The world wants wise mothers, as the true doctors of the race."

Many of his ideas were about religion, but out of that came a suffragette and abolitionist sentiment, which was standard to his policies in the state house and his family. How did I let myself become a slave to Johnny and not fulfill my voice, my dreams? Why couldn't I do more to fight back and be my own person? It felt good to help the people at the Quaker camp and to send articles to American journals about what was going on. I was finally being my Grandfather's child. I needed to be a product of all his struggles and carry them further.

In 1867, the Kansas legislature approved a proposed constitutional amendment granting women's suffrage. The Kansas State Legislature 1887, with Joel Moody as a part of the legislature, granted women the right to vote in municipal elections. From that time onward, the Women's Equal Suffrage Association staged several campaigns to sway the state Legislature to grant women full suffrage in state elections. Kansas women would be given full voting rights in 1912, before the passage of the national women's suffrage amendment in 1919. When I turned 18, I was able to vote. I had avoided the struggle and now, like so many, took it for granted, assuming that the fight was over. By the time I came of age in 1920, I proudly voted in the first national elections, which gave women those rights. My family of Quakers, my activist grandfather, nurtured my political sentiments. The Progressive journalism in the state also made me believe, like my grandfather, in the power of the pen.

I had kept boxes of letters and journals, and manuscripts to follow in Grandfather's footsteps. I was only 12 when he, a writer, politician, and war hero, died, leaving his letters and papers with my family. "I wanted to be like him, I declared. Oh, but wait, I can't. Be a lady, they said." My struggle to be treated equally and fairly was in my very being.

As I was coming of age, Kansas in the 1920s was a hotbed of Progressive politics. There wasn't one cohesive party but rather it was known for its free thought, rights of workers and farmers, rights of women. Women like Kate Richrds O'Hare was an iconic symbol of what a woman could be, do and say. People like the Moody family and from throughout the state including the Moody family, turned out to hear her Eugene V. Debs and were inspired by speeches that "Mother" Jones gave.

In the 1912 Presidential election, Eugene V. Debs won 7 percent of the vote for the Socialist Party, the largest for a third-party candidate at the time. The strongest area for him was in the southeast corner of the state of Kansas and Oklahoma, which was sometimes referred to as the Little Balkans. He fought for equal rights for all peoples and was a founding member of the IWW.

Journals such as the *Appeal to Reason*, led by J.A. Wayland and then Emanuel Haldeman Julius. These papers were extremely popular and helped to promote Debs' campaign and many other smaller elections. Its home was in the little town of Girard in the southeast corner of Kansas. It abutted Oklahoma, which led the nation in Socialist party members. It provided not only those in Kansas with human interest stories as well as political exposure, but also promoted Socialism and provided a place for writers such as Upton Sinclair. At its peak, it had a circulation of 750,000. After Haldeman-Julius took over the Appeal, he began to try to get literature and political doctrine out to a wider audience as well. He started what were called the Little Blue Books. They were the first small paperback books and included titles from Shakespeare to Sinclair Lewis as well as books about Buddhism, the Talmud, and Marxism. These very inexpensive books put knowledge in everyone's hands, believing that the education of the populace was the first weapon in equality of the classes and sexes.

The other critical journal of the time, for those interested or at least intrigued by Progressive politics was William Allen White's *Emporia Gazette*. White would come to head up the Journalism department at the University of Kansas in Lawrence, where I and Johnny, went to college and studied and learnt our trade. In 1923, he wrote "Letter to an Anxious Friend" which defended Freedom of Speech.

If I wanted to exist, to fight, to write, to find my voice, I had to find a way out. Find a way to be strong and move in a different circle from my sisters and mother. It would not always be a straight line, and this circuitous route was filled with potholes and missteps, but it was the story of my life. The first time that I remember actually breaking loose from the yoke of being "ladylike" was the summer that I took the job at the dude ranch in Wyoming. I stood up for myself to take this job in Paris, and now I survived nine months of war, bombings, and starvation with a child in tow. So, when I got Johnny's letter, I reminded myself of my background and knew that I would get home and make my way on my own. With this background, I knew that I could survive being on my own and walking my path. I would survive war, betrayal, and discrimination, and I could survive on my own. I know I can …maybe.

Chapter 10
Emeralds

Many things change in the course of a war, and we stop to think about our lives. Johnny's letter of December 17, 1939, arrived just before I got on the boat to leave Bourdeaux, six months after it was sent. Although the Quakers kept us fed and with a sense of purpose, I kept going to the American embassy in Bordeaux, hoping for help to get on a ship for America. I sometimes felt as if we would never get out, and yet we were told that if we didn't get out soon, we might end up in a concentration camp. The fear was elevated beyond the hunger. Suddenly, when I felt the most desperate, news came that our passports had been approved by the German authorities.

I had not had the luxury of going to an office, getting letters, or receiving money from Johnny or a paycheck before I got to Bourdeaux. When I got his letter from the embassy, I was afraid to open it, but bombs and starvation made that fear seem insignificant. I must admit that when I finally read it, I was shaken but not surprised.

The reality was that I did not at first want to go and take this job in Paris because the interruption was bound to interrupt the work that I had been doing for the magazines and my more creative writing of stories and plays, and because I was already tired. I just wanted to enjoy myself and do some new work. But it was a great opportunity to be a food editor in Paris. It seemed like a dream job, and Johnny had encouraged me to go. I agreed to go to Paris and took my own money out of the bank account for it. Johnny had assured me that it would be fine and he would be sending me money regularly while I was there. He quickly fell behind in the payments that were promised. And now, in the letters that I finally got to open after six months, he simply told me that he immediately wanted a divorce and wanted to marry Marjorie! No concern for us, no money, no compassion. Didn't he realize that even before the war was in full swing, Paris was not like before, and that everything cost much more? I had written in my letters to him, when we first arrived, how he had promised to send money so that Bobby could go to school in the Pyrenees, so that I could write uninterrupted. I told him how we didn't even have money now for proper furnishings. All we ever had was a mattress on the floor in our little apartment in Meudon. No wood for the fireplace, no good pillows or blankets. And Bobby was in the cheapest clothes. If I had access to my bank account and your money coming regularly, I would be in Paris instead of vegetating in Meudon. But, he wrote that instead of supporting his child, he would have to pay for the divorce and a new wife. I had written to him, back when I could get a letter out, to remember that Bobby was his son, also. I always skimped so that I could have a bank account for emergencies. Johnny never deprived himself and had to borrow from people, including me. A new wife would not be willing to skimp for your son.

He had said that he would replenish my savings account, and he never did. He said that if war broke out that he would send me more money, and never did. My friends in France told me to fly back and that they would give me the money to fly, that I must stop this divorce, and that Johnny couldn't file for desertion. He knew damn well that he sent me off to France. They kept saying, "Just refuse." I was sick and in a war zone, and all he cared about was pushing for a divorce. Several of my friends suggested that he knew Marjorie before he sent me off, and did this on purpose to get us out of the way. And suddenly, he wanted a quick divorce as I sat there sick, surrounded by bombings, food shortages, and steeped in physical and mental difficulties. All he could think of was himself.

The reality was that by 1936, well before I left for Paris, Johnny and I barely spoke. He would get various jobs, while I kept writing for whomever would take an article. I thought about the independence of Molly Brown and how I could change my life. Then my father died, and I went home to Kansas for a while before taking off for Paris. I dreamed about what my life might have been like if I had married one of the other suitors who had pursued me, or perhaps someone like Wilbur Phelps. The wonderful thing about writing was that I could change my reality to whatever I wanted. This was the story that I wrote about my alternate reality shortly before I left for Paris called Pansetta.

Pansetta

"I shook the sugar gown of tool white from its hanger. It had been 10 years since I had worn this dress, as it had been made for the junior prom and Karl, my first real boyfriend before Johnny. Karl had said that I was the prettiest girl on the floor that night. Funny that I should've run across it in the attic on the very day that Karl called her from his store once he learnt that I was back in town. Meeting by the side entrance of his store, he was undisturbed by the customers. "You look so good," he said, "Petunia, I suppose it ruins a girl's figure to have a baby, but not you." I didn't answer.

"Do you like New York?" he asked.

Abruptly, I responded in that cool, sure tone where he had just given me the facts that won't tell you anything. The very track which had exasperated me as a girl, I had asked myself then whether I could trust a man who always asked and never told. I had known he would be successful and rich, but I deliberately chose the man without a penny because he loved me so intelligently and completely, or so I thought.

I paused and half closed my eyes. I was a woman and a mother, now of a sturdy two-year-old boy. I had come home to rest and even decided on the way out that the rural woman on the train would put her hat on her lap as she rode the train back. I would put my best foot forward and be sweet and gracious about the life I now live. The minute someone said something cutting about me or my son, I would send a "ball of words" so hard and fast it would be impossible to return.

I finally answered Karl, saying, "I did so adore Paris." "Now, you are getting out of my depth," he looked down at her, "you have to stick to this continent. I can't talk to you at all about Paris. In NYC, did you live in the village? I know where the village is, it has all kinds of people." "What kind of people are there?" I asked. He stated mockingly, "Oh, artists and writers and actors, I mean wannabes." "I don't believe any good ones are there at all. I don't believe the real ones live there at all," I responded.

I asked if he knew Perry Street. "Well, no, I remember McDougal Street and…" I told him that Perry Street used to be where the stables were in the old days but they've been remodeled now. Jim Tony studied his Shakespeare in a room on Perry Street with Thornton Wilder and Jimmy Walker. I thought about my cute tiny apartment with its precious garden in the background so expensive but so necessary for the baby to have a place to play in the backyard.

He changed the subject and asked, "Did you get your degree? Didn't you want a PhD?" I replied. "My god, no, I didn't need it now I had the baby and Johnny's business to look after, and my writings." If you knew how terrible the last two years were, I thought to myself. We were only back in New York for a year. New York was big and complicated after Paris and bicycling, and Britney. I had to come home for a rest because I didn't see how I could get along there right now.

Karl asked, "How long are you staying?" So I smiled, and his hair crinkled away from his forehead the same way it used to. "Oh, I don't know yet." "Well, dance at the country club with me tomorrow night, and perhaps you'd better think about going to Kansas City with me Thursday and then on Friday…" If I had known there would be parties and holidays in the city, I probably would've managed to bring an evening gown or something from NYC. In New York, I could've found something cheap enough and slinky enough. How I wanted to look sophisticated after all these years away from my little college town. Silly isn't it to care, but I had such wonderful times when I was young, and it had been so long now since there had been any money for good times at all. Perhaps it was Karl who made me feel this way, a way that I never quite felt with Johnny. Karl, with his perfect taste in clothes, may have been an ideal father. Karl fit so perfectly into his father's shoes at the stores. His parents loved me, and they thought I was too exquisite for words. They would have given me practically all the brilliant accessories I needed to marry their son.

His family appreciated that I didn't have much money, but that I made all the most beautiful dresses all by myself. This white dress I made for prom was perfect for Karl. Then, like an Oklahoma cyclone, Johnny walked into my life. I never wore the white dress again. Johnny would say I hate you in white. He said it again in Paris once or twice when I considered copying an August Bernard Paris dress that was in white.

What should I do? In a flash, it came to me. I straightened up, cheeks flushing with old-time joy and creativity. I would make a quaint little empire dress out of the old white dress with a high, tight bodice that would never show any old belly bulge. I would make one of those short jackets like at Lord and Taylor's. Then add some brilliant colors like Crimson and turquoise. Crimson, of course, and make the sleeves much larger, poof! And then I said, "Yes, I think I can do that." And I thought that I could do one of those adorable taffeta bags like the Russians were always making in Paris. He would never know that it was the same dress that I had worn with him those many years ago.

By the time I had shopped for the material and made the little jacket and bag, my nerves were tight. At 4 o'clock, I took a bath and tried to go to rest. Then suddenly, in came a little boy's excited commands. He wanted to play with one of the rabbits and to build a home, and then a castle and a railway. Can we, can we? Marge came to the door with a disgusted look on her face. "Say, Sue, if you finished your sewing, you think that you might entertain that son of yours, he's a little too much for me."

I went and asked Ruth if she would watch Billy for me. "No, I've got some work to do, you take care of your child." "You finished your sewing! What's happened to you? I thought you came home to rest," her father said. "No, I guess not," her father looked puzzled. I just thought maybe you had to go to bed instead of running around with Karl while you were here. He rose angrily and picked up his hat. "… but I don't know what you came home for, and I'm not going to stay around here while you make a perfectly happy family quarrelsome. You better not see to much of Karl, that's all, he's no damn good." The old man stomped off the porch and down the sidewalk. But there were the pure facts. Lawrence had not changed one hundredth of 1 inch while I was gone. Seven years had left no mark on it, not one wrinkle of whatever it was that made people tolerant and happy and bubbling over with *joie de vivre*. Johnny was right when he warned me that this old-fashioned little town would not like the fact that she was coming back without her husband. "If I can't go home to my family, why have one." There was nothing left to do but take the baby out to play until suppertime, and perhaps I could rest for 15 to 20 minutes while they ate. And then she would just eat some of her meal later and get dressed.

"Come on, Bobby, shall we go for a walk?" Let's go see the tractor, mommy. It makes the biggest noise!" He pushed his hand into mine and walked out the door to the street, where it was being paved. We passed by an elderly woman, a friend of my mother's, whom she sat with when she was alive. They ate on the front porch, and I watched as they discussed the tax rate that they would now have to pay for the pavement. I nodded in a friendly way. "Oh, Sue," called one, "Come show us the baby?"

I walked with Bobby up the path to the walkway. One of them said, "I always remember you, dear, when you first came to a Sunday dinner. Grandmother O'Brien said you were so good." The other one was talking baby talk to Bobby. I just wanted to walk on. And they asked me all about Paris, how I liked France. I scarcely remember answering them before they were showing a

French plate that a brother had sent them some 25 years before. I acknowledged the plates politely, then the books, and the furniture, admired them all 1000 times. Then they told me of the extremely expensive electric refrigerator that she bought and how it should be made to produce a much larger quantity of cubes, and the cost could be rationalized because of the production of a quart of ice cream made from the cubes. I was not quite following the conversation. I was occupied with helping to keep my son's sticky, dirty fingers away from the books.

"How long will you be here?" "I don't know, maybe a week, maybe a year, I really haven't decided," I replied. She looked at me strangely with that kind of answer the old ladies were irritated by, "goodbye" I smiled and said, "Do hope the refrigerator turns out to be satisfactory?"

Bobby was squirming to return to the bulldozers and construction. I picked him up and he was happy there in my arms, hugging his warm little body close to mine with unsteady elbows digging into me. I hurried down the street, out of view of the women, to spend the rest of the time on the swings and teeter-totter ring with him in the park. I was very tired by the time I dressed for the party, but hopefully very beautiful. My extremely successful dress had even the nieces glowing with admiration. Before I knew it, Karl came springing up the walkway in a cream-colored linen suit, a new kind of tie with Mexican plaid stripes. His dark, wavy hair gave him the conquering look. He looked at me and just said, "Wonderful!" "It was toxic to be held with such exuberance after being one of many in the city and my mothering life." He breathed hard, pulling his arm through mine in the old way. "I knew you would do something to make them all look like country girls. I like you that way, and I can dance a straight program with you tonight, and I never have to stop?" "This is the same town, that is the same family. It's only you that has changed, just say heck so I don't have to keep an eye on you. This is Mr. Mink from Adams. Sue, he's driving out with us. It won't be too crowded, I hope." Karl started the car, and when they were well down the street, he pulled me very close. I was faintly annoyed to find the crisp sleeves of my jacket crushed. The evening had a soft sky and steely clouds. There was a gentleness in the air that was faintly disturbing after the stimulating iodine winds of a coastal city. They drove up over the hill, down again, and up the next one. I turned to look back at the hills to imagine a Britney coastline castle against the sky. It was just a big farmhouse.

I wiggled away from Karl, so he grinned and said, "Don't wiggle." I said to him, "I will wiggle if I want to." "We all know you think it's pretty out here, and you know what I'm thinking of doing when Mac leaves us, persuading you to stay a while in the car." They swung into the country club driveway. There were Japanese lanterns everywhere. I felt as young as a white tulle frog and "like a split personality", inwardly wishing I could have napped before coming or had a cocktail offered by my father. Mac left them, and they sat in the car for a minute. "I have some whiskey," said Karl. "I'd offer you a drink, but I don't think you better." I felt disturbed by his comment. Karl lifted me out of the car as he would have pulled her from a stone wall on a hike; it was his old way. He kissed the top of my head, that was Karl's way, too. And then they danced. I had forgotten how divinely he danced. Perhaps he danced better than he had 10 years ago, I could not tell because it was so intoxicating, to be floating again. Toward midnight, we sat under the big old weeping willow tree; by moonlight under a very faint translucent moon on this first night of renewed acquaintance. Karl sat on the ground and stretched his long legs. "My darling princess, you are too young and beautiful. I could dance forever, but tomorrow I could never get back to work, and the old man thinks it's time I get over my wild oats, what he calls pleasure. If I don't stay fit while you are here, he will go on the warpath, and it will be the end for me. You will have to divorce your husband and marry me, I'm warning you." "Don't take the tragic view, Karl." I laughed, and he turned as he looked longingly at me.

My hands were in my lap, and Karl came and put his hands lightly on top of them. "I know about this dress now. I was too young to know before, then I remembered all at once. You always thought of things more gradually." The magic witchery of the violin floated out to them. Dan Starling was singing. His voice caressed her, his shoulder against mine said that we would sit here all night. How tragically tender that voice. It was always some boy who could sing love songs that tapped at and caressed my heart.

How was it that Karl had his arm around my shoulder, kissing my hair, and I thought that I should put my hands up as if to push him away. But he held them too tightly as he looked at me there in the moonlight. Softly now, voices singing came in, the violin on the other side was like the breeze, shimmering white leaves above their heads. "Let's dance," I said. Karl led me straight across the lawn a little ahead of me. I felt young again and completely alluring. It was certainly a magical evening.

It was nearly noon when I woke up the next day. Bobby must've been out of the house, I thought with relief, as I turned over. I gradually smelled the whiff of baking bread from the kitchen. I pulled on my robe, tingling with anticipation. One of Aunti's sugar rolls with a cup of coffee… how perfect and two big, beautiful Kansas eggs with her 2nd cup. But Auntie was definitely cross with me, as she pulled out one of the pans from the oven.

She sat it down with a bang on the table and a roll. I asked in my tiniest voice, "A sugar roll, Auntie, dear?"

"Don't call me, dear. I didn't make any rolls. You better not stay out so late if you want to get up with your baby. Ruth has other work to do. Today was her watch day." I made arrangements with Ruth last night, and I turned back and began to toast myself some bread. Soon, my father came in. "Aren't you early for lunch?" I tried to talk to him, but he seemed so worried and did not answer.

Marge arrived, tousled her hair, and her bright eyes from a long sleep. "What, no sugar rolls?" she marked, giving me a sly look. "Where do you think you are, at the Ritz? So we should be serving you breakfast in bed, huh?" "Don't start that French stuff," said my father, slamming his paper down. "That's probably what's the matter with her living with those degenerates till she doesn't know how to behave when she finds herself back in a nice decent town again." Something about Karl and Karl's father and all their mutual friends was worrying her father. I munched my toast thoughtfully and tried to think of a funny story. "Dad," tentatively I began to speak, "did you ever hear of the Frenchman who came to live in a little town in America and couldn't find a satisfactory cook until he came across an old Chinese man."

Auntie plopped another pan of bread onto the table and snapped, "I suppose women are just like men in Paris, they go out with other people and then come home to cover up their tracks with nasty stories." I got up without folding a napkin and went to my room. Sunlight was touching the flowers on an arrangement of glass shelves and white iron. It was the room she had always had. It had become even lovelier over the decades as she had added quilts and rugs, and flowers. How heavenly just to have rested and had a good time, but I could see there would be no rest for me in this house. Still, perhaps if I stood by my ideas as I had always done in the past, despite what anyone would say, I could have a proper holiday.

Marge, my niece, came into the room. "I'll tell you what. You can go ahead and take your trip to Kansas City even if the house falls, and I will watch your kid. Believe me, I have had to go through this longer than you have. I had two beaus last year and only one of them with any money in the bank. I chose that one about the time they got to the place where they said, "You can love any man, darling, and if you can love a rich one much easier than a poor one. They brought up your case, and I haven't got anyone I love right now. I don't even love you, though I did last year when they told me things about you. But I'll watch the kid if you'll take me with you next time you go to the city. I'm so sick of this town and this family, and I can offer to hire out as a governess and forget all about the degree… if I didn't hate children. I would!"

"All right, I will take you next time," I said. "I will take you today if I had any money to make it right with someone else and give her the rest. She doesn't like kids either. No one does. And yet what's eating dad right now is the idea I ought to be having more children if I'm true to my husband."

I felt a shade better putting some Bonwit Teller moisturizer on my face. I pulled out the most winsome hat I had in Lawrence, and would then feel better once I put that on. It was a little piece, and I put it under the crown in the back to make it fit forward. None of the other girls in town knew anything about hats, and that it had an almost invisible, slight rubber cord edging to hold it past my head at this year's precise angle. My plain Vionnet coat was now old but still more elegant than any in this town. It was a flowing bias-cut wool fabric that was all the style in NY and Paris.

Karl got the car, and we were off to Kansas City. He said, "I want to see you with your hat off, please take your hat off, I just want to see your cock curls. It's been a whole 24 hours since I kissed them, and I felt slightly nauseated missing you." I replied, "We are too old to be acting silly." "You don't believe me when I say I love you," he insisted, "you forget what you used to mean to me," as he started kissing my hands again and again, "please stay here, I can't live any longer without you."

And what should I do with Bobby? I asked. "He can go to boarding school, we all went to boarding school, my God, sweetheart, you think too much about that little boy." My mouth got too tight at the corners. It was true usually, but now I didn't think a lot about Bobby, in a rather abnormal way perhaps, but how can I help it with no money, no news from my husband, and a family constantly nagging? "If we don't go on to Kansas City, and if you are going to stop the car every two minutes, I should just cry and make a scene, and ask the first person who passes to take me back to Lawrence." "Don't be a little idiot." Karl smiled, and his smile was tired too. "I'll take you out in a minute. I just want to ask you something. Does your husband still love you?" "Yes," I said. "Well, so do I. " Then he was silent for a while, and Karl drove very fast until he said, "You've been hearing lots about me from that kid niece of yours, and part of it is true and part of it isn't. I have had a good time as bachelors do, but I'm not as rotten as they say. I couldn't be as successful as I am, and I'm a rather successful man, my dear, you know it would do you lots of good to marry me."

I was silent on the road ahead of them, and the smoky planes were filled with changing bales of color. "I'm just going to turn up a side road here for a minute. There's a place full of Apple blooms, and you'll see what a magnificent view there is from the river." My heart stopped at the beauty stretched before me. Karl sat quietly. "I own this. Someday I'm going to build the kind of house my wife will love." Then he turned and drove on when they were nearly to the city, and he wheeled into another side road. "If you don't mind, we won't go anywhere in public. There's a little place out here where they dance to a 23-piece orchestra. Would you mind if I keep something like you so precious all to myself?"

I felt like a young girl again, and I dropped my hat onto the bench along the wall and let Karl put his coat somewhere else. It was a cozy English sort of place with checkered tablecloths, the tables set in stalls along the wall, and benches on one side comfortably tufted. I knew I looked wistful and graceful in my long skirt. It made me more ladylike and decorative than the other girls. Karl nodded to another corner. He was in his perfect setting. Six feet in height in a dashing wardrobe. He was my complement in his stylish simplicity. Yes, we would have been ideal mates. The other girls were all eyes and noisy. Their companions talked in a loud voice as they ordered more beer.

"Do you mind if I take milk?" asked Karl, leaning forward and shutting the door from her view. "I'm not drinking anymore at all. It isn't because of the accident you heard about. It's because I drank too much in my time, and I want to be as young as you now. I'll just stick to milk and be the safest thing. . ."He held her eyes with his own and told her again that he loved her.

I told Karl to just have half a bottle of beer, "You must," I said. The orchestra began soft strains of Sweetheart, You Drive Me Mad. Karl pulled me close and they danced out onto the wide veranda, "My darling, darling Pansetta," he whispered. I shook my shoulder free and laughed at him. I thought, how can this sweetness last? The tenor voice again came wharfing in. How can I hold you fast, so sweet?" Karl's head was so close that I could feel the rhythm of his breath. He held my chin and called me, "Sweet little one. I'm really being hypnotized." I told him over the beer, "You do not realize how hypnotizing you are. But I did not come home to choose a new husband. I came home to rest." He spoke very softly, "Remember how things travel into space. I know, darling, you did not come home to rekindle an old fire. I know you had almost forgotten me. But not quite." He looked at her confidently. "And I won't go on without you." "You could never have left Johnny if you had loved him the way you love me. I have everything for happiness except you. Now, in a little while, I am going to have you. Little white dress, little white dress, will you wear the little white dress to a wedding?"

It was early the next morning when Bobby came running into my bed. "Mommy, where is daddy?" he asked. "I wanna go on a bus to daddy," he said. The words were said in a parent-like way and contained and came from one of the adults, prompting him to say that. "Grandfather says we better see daddy." I slammed the bathroom door and began brushing my teeth. I could hear them at breakfast below, and Auntie's shrill voice. I stared out, looking at the window, at the tulips in bloom below. They were deep red, my favorite color. This was her mother's house, this was her own home, and now that I had become a lawfully wedded wife, it held no place for me. There was no room in this, in this territory, for a woman who had married and then maybe married the wrong man and then came back for the visit. It would've been the same no matter whom she had chosen. Perhaps it was nothing more or less than the circumstances of doing something unusual, of returning to rest, and then instead of sleeping all the time or concentrating on making her child a little show off. That was probably it, the old people resented her because they had long ceased to play. The young ones because they wanted to. But the fact remained as she hung up her towel, there was no place for her here. She was Mrs. Johnny White. She had not come home again to choose between Karl and her husband. If she was being pushed into some wobbly state of mind, which might happen, but she told Karl last night. He insisted that he had wanted her for years. I knew in my heart that his reactions were largely conditioned by his family and his loneliness. Also, she was certainly more appealing as a well-travelled person. She was appealing and dangerous and everything but the rather simple home safe girl who would come back for a while to visit. "Sue… I wish she would come to breakfast," called out Ruth. "I want to get the dishes done so I can go to the country with dad for eggs." I struggled down the stairs, wishing I felt a little more cheerful. Her father was cross and scolding about his coffee. "Will you take Bobby with you?" she asked, thinking to make him happy by being with his grandson. "I certainly will not," he shouted. Do you think I want to spend good money on eggs and then have them bust? You better start going to bed earlier so you can get up and take care of your baby!" "I'm not going to be bothered with him today," announced Ruth "I've got too much to do" and "I'm not either," said auntie, "because I think it's disgraceful the way you're getting the whole town to talk and I don't have to hesitate to say so."

Marge jumped up from the table turning over oatmeal dish and not caring what splattered. As she ran upstairs a voice floated back "making a mess of things , sure I'll confess …" And suddenly, I heard the door slam. I didn't even know what that was all about.

Somehow, everyone left the kitchen, and Auntie went to pull out the dandelions, and I was left alone with some cold coffee and rather stiff toast. Bobby sat on the floor in the living room, quiet for the moment, building a boat from some new blocks his father had bought for him at the station. She heard the postman, and I went desperately to see whether there was a letter or any money. Both were there, and I sat in a little heap on the couch to read that my husband missed me too much to write and hoped I was well. He wanted her and their beautiful son to enjoy all the splendors and beauty of the hills and valleys and life-giving sunshine. In a swift panorama, the landscape of the ride to Kansas City came to her mind. Karl's eyes and Karl's arms, and the beautiful hilltop with waving white branches.

Bobby kicked his boat and said, "Let's go outdoors, mommy." "Are you going to the Beta house tonight?" Marge asked me. "All of my family just seems to be standing around criticizing my frock, criticizing my curls, thinking of me as a vulgar person, not liking whoever I choose to watch Bobby. I shivered. "I think I'll have to pack and leave right away for New York."

Marge's voice was shocked. "Why, why on earth, what has happened?" "Nothing, I just think I'll be going home. Marge leapt down the stairs and said, "Then take my advice and get out of here by noon on the bus before they get back. They'll think you have sinned. Let him think it out of your sight." In the perfect frenzy, I packed, I scrubbed up Bobby, and put his dirty clothes in one bag.

His clean ones are in another drawer at the door. I kissed Marge. "I'll call Karl, maybe he'll be mad enough to take me! You left your white dress and taffeta jacket. Can I keep them? I'll never wear them, I'll just treasure them to remember your sweet small visit home, and if I marry Karl, please don't come to the wedding. For God's sake, let this be a lesson to you, and don't even write to them." Bobby and I were far in the depths of the taxi. Marge screamed out, "But you can send me any cast-off dads you like."

Bobby and I were so tired by the time we got home to our tiny NYC apartment. We sat by the tiny fireplace that cast such lovely light in the small apartment. When I arrived, Johnny had come to the door in slippers, too dazed to realize what had happened. They had put the baby to bed and in less time than it usually takes. They were alone at last. "It's no good, Johnny," looking out at the pieces of manuscript littering the room–– "but maybe it will be now." He leaned over to kiss her, then caught her close and kissed her long, and I kept my face near his. "Isn't it chilly here for the end of April?" stay there Johnny said, and he put the three logs remaining into the fireplace.

"We've got to make these last all night. I'm going to get you some supper, don't you dare move," she heard the coffee perking in the kitchen, too tired to think. I wondered whether Johnny was cooking something up. There was the aroma of toasted cheese floating through the narrow hallway. He had probably lived on cheese and cigarettes and coffee, the whole time I was gone. "Poupee?" Yes. "Are you glad to be back? Yes. Are you glad to be back, oh darling, it's so heavenly to have you home," he snorted, "wait, don't let me burn this toast."

And then Johnny whispered in my ear, smothering me with kisses as I gasped for breath. Then he said, "We have a new roadster!" "Why? What on earth do you mean?" I said. My boss' wife wanted me to watch the house and water her bird. I've been doing it, and then she just gave me the car and doesn't need it back! She doesn't want it back now that she can't afford a chauffeur. So, isn't that the most beautiful thing you've ever heard of, and we can go to the country every week, when it doesn't rain. And then burst out and then have our own house before very long." Johnny went to the kitchen and returned with a beautiful Russian tray they had found on sale for $.69. "Oh that blessed tray with coffee and cheese and toast."

But that was just the story in my head. Two weeks later, we were off for America, through Spain, and then Portugal, and finally our farewell by boat to Lisbon. Leaving behind Mitzie and Lisette, and Renee, and the sound of bombs, and our emaciated stomach. Finally, we were on a boat heading home. We returned from war and famine, and the reality was that Johnny didn't even meet us at the boat. No toast and cheese, no fireplace, no kisses. Nothing. We were alone to figure out our world. There were no Slayer of Dragons to come to the rescue. I was the only one who could slay my dragons.

Chapter 11
The Clasp

"We sat there, your son and the woman that you promised to love forever, forlorn, sick, malnourished, fearful, surrounded by bombings, starving, in profound physical and mental difficulties AND all you could write to us is how you suddenly want a quick divorce. How heartless and cruel. Incredible. What kind of person does that to someone in the middle of a war? "You are not the slayer of dragons but you are the dragon."

On the other hand, I did not want to be married to Johnny either. We were unhappy for so many years. I have known for 2 or 3 years that you were not happy and you were drinking more. And the more you drank the meaner you became. But I thought that when I came back, we might be renewed, rejuvenated, and miss each other. We drifted and many things that you like to do, I do not. You made it clear that you would not change for me. I liked to plan and you were impulsive. And Bobby, of course, felt the tension in the house and became naughty. So I wrote back, "Go and get re-married and be happy and leave me alone, as long as your financial commitment to us does not fall behind. I also want to get divorced, but not until I come back, and get myself together, get well again, and when we can figure out the finances. How can you rush this now with my current situation? It is beyond inconsiderate." I was just so furious. "And what about Bobby. At least think of him. He has been through so much this year. Fear, bombings, seeing death, destruction, and being hungry all the time. It was no time or place to be a young boy, and he looks forward to seeing you, and now I must tell him that you are divorcing us? I have to explain to Bobby that we will not all be together. He still seems to think that we will all get together and do things, go on vacations together. He really doesn't understand. I had to tell him that men never kiss their first wife again when they have a second wife, but that we would always be friends. I told him that he would see you for long vacations, or if there is a time when I really need a break. How can I be worrying about this after all we have been through? We are escaping war-torn France and starvation. Don't you understand? How can you do this to us?"

Once you are a divorced woman, everyone assumes that you are fast and loose and just want to get married again. In Paris or NYC, alone with a young boy was normally difficult, but as a divorced woman was worse. "And what about our house that we worked so hard to get. I didn't want our house in Teaneck, NJ sold. I want a home to come back to." I told Johnny that he could live there with Marjorie until I got back. With all the troubles in the world, I just wanted to know that my house was there for us to come back to. We moved around so much for your jobs, and I had lost out completely on my writing. I have not had any fun at all for the last 5 years. I have lost so many tangible and intangible things. I deserve to enjoy life now. I needed to do for myself now, finally. I needed to remember Molly Brown and my heritage, the strength of my grandfather. I needed to go back to being that girl who tamed wild horses. *No, I want to be the wild horse.*

But first I needed to hunt down a good lawyer through the snow and ice, and us still ill. You might just have to wait. Bobby kept having bouts of Bronchitis. We really should head south for some warmth and sunshine when we get back, but we needed some money for the trip. And I couldn't afford anyone to help clean up Bobby's constant mess. I wrote, "I want complete custody of my boy, complete rearing and direction of him now. Otherwise, I will never consent to the divorce."

Johnny and Marjorie wrote to me that they were upset with the slowness of my response. How dare they! I was in France, where there was a war all around me, and they were worried about how quickly they could get married! Did he think that I started the war on purpose? I was doing what I could in my time in a very difficult situation. It would be so much nicer if they just waited until I returned. "I move slowly now as Bobby and I are sick, and this is certainly an emotional strain. It is why I don't break dishes because I cannot afford to replace them, I don't buy new dresses, and have to spend extra hours food shopping and searching for things during these difficulties." There was hardly time to go to the typewriter. The mail was coming very slowly as well. A letter dated January 27 from Johnny arrived February 13, and in it, you actually asked me for a return cable by February 2nd! My first of the month money has not arrived yet either. Where was that?

"Considering that for years I put my happiness on the side, and you kept saying that you were happy." Johnny was only concerned about his circumstances and having to wait, while Bobby and I were in real dire circumstances and wondered if his money would come late or not at all. We would have starved if I had not put money aside. "I do not have enough money to come home, if I could find passage, and certainly could not afford a hospital if I needed it. I need time to do the things legally with my lawyer. Remember how much I managed the funds and contributed my earnings towards major expenses like a car, furnishings, and the Teaneck house. I rarely bought things for myself, but whatever I bought for me or Bobby, I generally used my own earnings." Johnny worried so much about his honeymoon, while I worried about bombings from Germany and the Russians in retaliation. "If you move into the house until I return, please take care of the furniture. It took us so long to be able to afford it. Remember that I love that blonde table. And cover the library table with a sheet so that it doesn't get scratched."

"Think about what you are doing. When we first met, we thought that everything was perfect, and I was the pretty girl with curls down her back. And you swore that you could never be unhappy with me. Later, I was the wife that you said men at the office found unsympathetic to her husband. All because I was conscious of managing our budget, because you did not."

"We signed a contract, a vow, and it is not something to be taken lightly. We talked about having children. We discussed the consequences before we married, and about my working. How could I have married you, so poor and in debt, for that matter, if I had not some assurances?" It would have been better to marry the rich guy from Lawrence, then to have stepped off blindly into a marriage that was never a marriage, but only something that you could toss over with a shake of the head at the first new girl who came along when we might have been suffering from a quarrel. You said to me, "I have not been happy with you, darling." I just rolled my eyes and looked off to the moon. "I know damn well that you are not happy and I know that lots of our unhappiness came from you as much as from me. It serves no purpose to list all the ways that you made me unhappy, flirting with other girls, drinking, spending money foolishly, but it will only make us all upset.

The reality is that Bobby and I are over here somewhere in France. Where you sent us. We can't exist if you desert us. And I will not to be able to just go into any office for a job. People frown on divorced women. And you told people and family that it was my idea and that that was why we are now getting divorced!!

Send me the extra $200 so that we can go south for our health and pay for a lawyer. Also, have in your agreement that your office will send me the money. In the end, perhaps I was too ambitious for you. You need another sort of girl who would be better to just worry about you."

In my last letter, before I got on the boat, I wrote: "Send the papers and I will sign them."

I made it very clear to Johnny that I would never marry again. I wouldn't ever want the responsibilities again of another man's life. Fifteen years of that had wasted my accomplishments and flowering as a writer. The least I could now expect for myself after having given up my career, having a baby, taking care of financial matters, and depriving myself, was complete peace of mind and to enjoy some small moments with friends, sit by the lake, walk through the woods, and write without restrictions. Even if I did conceivably fall in love, never again would I give up my life for a man.

I had such a great job bug before I left for France, but now, I was just so exhausted. What kind of job could I get as the mother of a rambunctious young boy, and divorced? And from being ill and malnourished for so long, I looked like an aged grandmother.

"I consented because you said that your job was at risk, and your hectic, desperate message about losing your shirt financially. So, I didn't want to hang you out there, but it must be clear that all decisions about Bobby are mine."

Then, on May 6, 1940, Johnny wrote to me:

"Well, darling—it is all over. The courtroom was hot and sticky and full of flies and the smell of stale cigars. My lawyer waddled around, and your spry little banty rooster waddled after him. The Chancellor grinned and chewed tobacco and said nothing that I could hear. Presently, they motioned to come to me, and we went down in the elevator and out into the warm, clean spring air. That is the way they settle these matters between people who have loved and wept and struggled together for almost a generation. Thank God, it is over!

I walked up the mountain and sat for a long time, remembering. I remembered the mountain on which we sat, you and I, in Estes park, planning what we would do in this world — the walks down by the muddy river at the foot of Ohio street --- the morning strolls in Montsouris. Why did it turn out like this, Sudy? You were so fine and brave and beautiful! And honest. So, I shall remember it always, trying not to remember the times I let you down. You were such a splendid wife to me. Together, we made such a splendid lad. Is that altogether a failure?"

I just wrote back that I never wanted to see Marjorie, didn't want her around my son. I didn't want to see Johnny. "If you want to see Bobby, you will wait outside to pick him up."

Johnny's job in Washington, DC, of course, proved unsatisfactory, and he now had reduced wages. He wanted me to move to a cheaper rent! He wrote, "But wouldn't it be better to go on living in a decent part of town?" "We can't move to the slums, you know, with the baby," I declared. I couldn't do any more than I was. The rent simply ate up everything. Having different people come to take care of Bobby was almost the same amount of money as a maid. He replied, "All right, get a maid then." I reiterated, "But we won't move, I'll tell you that," the whole question was always the money involved. "We will go bankrupt then, but don't change his address."

The only way that I could work was to get a maid/babysitter for when Bobby was not in school. I hired a pretty little Swedish thing, refined and sentimental. She could cook when she felt like it. Bobby was growing up fast and would play for hours alone, creating a set of blocks which he named something extravagant like the Temple Ogre. I never seemed to know what he was saying, probably because I didn't know what she was teaching him. He clung to me whenever I came home. I never knew what residual feelings he had from the war. He didn't want to talk about it, so we reverted to baby talk and song singing:

"This little piggy went to the market/ this Little piggy went home…."

At first, I thought that a maid would solve my problems. It was August, and a cool wind swept into my nostrils as I pulled the door open and left. All I wanted to think about was that anyone who could work for me should love Bobby, and she could be trained. Then, I thought that perhaps Johnny would decide to spend more time with his son, even if he didn't have him much. I just wanted Bobby and Johnny to see each other occasionally for dinner, and I wanted them both to realize that I was a wonderful mother. Johnny must know I did love him and still think of him as Bobby's father. For a while, the money came from Johnny, and then the checks became intermittent. They stopped. I scarcely knew where to turn.

Eventually, I found an advertising position in a large store. I attacked the position with all intensity. It was in a sad little building across the street from a sturdy Italian building, which might have been lovely in the old days with flower boxes. I loved looking out at it. At one time, it had the most magnificent hand-carved stairway brought in there by James Gordon Bennett. Once he had brought the old stairway back from Italy because he thought it was so beautiful, and installed it in his office building. I would go to look at it during my lunch break. I wanted to just stroll down it like a Princess, carried away by my Prince, but no! Fairy tales are not true, and it was just a stairway. I had to come back to reality. There was no more room in my life for those fairy tales. They were all lies that men told you to trap you.

The reality was that I stood on the street looking at the sad state of the Square where the Herald used to be. The building across the way was filled with men's ties, socks, and topcoats.

It was one of the gloomiest days in New York. As the snow was melting, it soon turned to a soft rain with muddy streets. I watched a big yellow truck sway beneath the elevated trains. Music soared in the air all around me. It was a radio car advertising the airing of a program for children. It drove up and down the street! It played Little Piggy Went to Market. Bobby loved to have his toes wiggled after his bath. But the babysitter never did this. She bathed him quickly, put him into his bathrobe, and tucked him into bed.

I found myself sitting very straight, gazing at a little boy on the street. This was not the life I wanted. I was not with my son, I was not writing, and I was divorced. I was no longer writing articles; I was back where I was more than a decade ago. And poor Bobby was becoming so tired and lonely that none of the maids helped. Suddenly, I was propelled out of my thoughts when, from around the corner, a radio car came swerving. This one was white, following a taxi from the hospital. I wore my old dark blue coat and held it tightly around my neck as I hurried over to Fifth Avenue.

It was too expensive to go to the cafeteria in the building for lunch because the food there was extravagantly good, in a beautiful space, and you paid for that. Although the building was lovely. The colonnade was newly decorated, trying to look like the days of the Ritz in Paris. But in the basement of the five and dime, there was a lunch counter. I could just sit there and eat my lunch and cheer up. It was so nice to be by myself and be served, if just for a bit of time. There was a special lunch for 25 cents each week.

This week, the meat special was pork, or they had a hot roast beef sandwich for 15 cents, and you could have any of the desserts for ten cents if you like pears with ice cream and chocolate sauce. It was so good. I ate my sandwich slowly, while an old lady looked across the way, delicately picking out the fruit from the ice cream.

The girl behind the counter looked again as I asked for change from a quarter. When she gave me a dime, she smiled and pushed a nickel back at me. I slipped the nickel gratefully into a coin purse. How fearfully important nickels were right then. She thought they were symbolic of the differences between despair and a glimpse of our future.

Eventually, I was given a raise in my new job. It helped to fill the breach from Johnny's payment, but was strengthened by the knowledge that my work was good.

"My God, you haven't touched one garment in the copy, and it must be ready for the news by noon," said my boss, Mr. Mills. He tried to glare at me, but reached out to my right hand instead. "I'm not going to scold you, but I have to school that other girl until I'm horse. I think you're planning to have a rotten Christmas, just like me, and get this work finished. The girls' snowsuits must be sold immediately because I don't think that there will be more than one snowstorm this winter. They like to blame the advertising department for things not selling, but perhaps it's really just the buyer, buying too much. I guess I can't tell the buyer that, so you must get the art department to draw the snow suits in such a way that mothers would really want them. A little girl with a snowman and a Christmas suit or a rabbit for Easter."

I looked at him for a moment to say, "I will have copy ready by noon. I was standing there thinking. I told the artist to draw the child in an unconventional fortress."

Everyone made such a hullabaloo in my office if you were late at all, but this morning, my Bobby was coughing and I had to take more time with him than usual. Consequently, I came down to the office with my hair looking wild. Mr. Goldstein, my immediate superior, looked at me momentarily and actually complimented my hair. After a moment, he seemed a little less severe. "You better put your little head on. Go to the washroom now, and fix your hair so that Mr. Miller will not see you. And come in here to work by noon, sit at your machine until you get that copy out, then have lunch and drop by until three. I'll be back later today."

I returned to work and went to the large copy room, where they all typed. I was surprised to find Mr. Goldstein there. He was talking on the phone to Elsie. "Yes, my dear Miss Bloom, yes, yes, oh, I am certain you have done your best now, when you're finished, please come straight back to the office." He nodded to me and walked quickly ahead out of the room. He went into another office that he reserved for private conversations, and led me to a small typewriter table. "Will you please go immediately to the men's shop to inspect our new suits? We need a three-column-wide ad, and slightly amusing because my column will be next to it. Yours is the one they've approved." They, the buyers, decided to run your personal shoppers ad!

Suddenly, a career in this nice little store wasn't so bad, I thought. It was as if I'd been dressing in a drab brown gown and suddenly had been handed a Parisian coat. Three months later, I was feeling good, hurrying up Madison Avenue. I had that Saturday off. It was such a joy to be out in the sunshine, leaving Bobby early, well fed, and in his sandbox with a babysitter. I was looking for a hat shop where they copied French models. The hats at the store have been frightful lately, and the buyer told me, "If you will design a few of your type, have them made up by Elaine, and then let us copy them, I will pay the bill," he announced.

I began to work on them in earnest, hoping that it could bring me some real additional income.

I finished designs that were perfect, and then crawled onto the bus across the Queensborough Bridge just as the sunset was painting a magic background. How good to come home early and to a clean apartment, Bobby content after a delicious supper. I was tired of staying at work late at night, and I didn't sleep well now, but there was no extra money for movies or seeing many of my friends, anyway. I was looking forward to having a good time with my boy when they got home to our little apartment.

Meanwhile, Marie took the bus to the children's nursery school. Bobby had started going there where he felt less lonely. But immediately whenever she picked him up, Bobby would say, "Where's mommy? Where is mommy? Isn't mommy coming?" Marie never answered. She said that by night, she was tired of answering questions. When he got home that day, I yelled out, "Bobby, boy, here, here I am. Bobbie boy." There was a loud squeal, but then he said, "Where is daddy? Is daddy coming tonight?" She bit her lip. Every night over six months, he would ask about a daddy who did not come. Long ago, letters infrequently arrived, and he was talking fast and excitedly, his eyes bright, his cheeks crimson. But as she looked around the room, she could scarcely understand what he said. The disorder that she walked into in her apartment made her stomach feel quite ill. Her bedroom slippers were in the dusty corner with Bobby's muddy boots, and the ones that should've been cleaned yesterday were in another corner. And her only comfortable chair had

Bobby's dear little bedroom shoes. There were rolls of lint under her bed. How had I not noticed this before? Did I always get home too late to care? "Marie," I called to the babysitter. My voice was shrill. "Come here." In a moment, the girl stuck her head around the door. Marie had changed her plain Kathryn Hepburn bangs and cut her hair. Turned out that instead of playing in the sun earlier in the day, Bobby spent hours in a beauty parlor. He always acted up when he had afternoons indoors. She had then dropped him off at the day school since it was a Saturday.

"Marie, you must keep my bedroom and Bobby's shoes clean. I can't go on telling you about everything." "Well, you see, I'm going out tonight, and Bobby was awful today. I could hardly get him home with the food." "You have to plan things out, Marie, it isn't hard, you're going to have to think this thing out really, if you are, if you want to keep your job." Marie shot back, "I was over to the agency today, and Miss Smith said that she needs lots of girls for industrial work now, and it pays better than this. I don't know – of course, I'm crazy about Bobby. . ."

"Do I smell meat burning? She stood there, silent, insolent, "For heaven's sake, take it off the stove." The door banged, and I began to pick up the shoes. My coral mules with golden heels that Johnny bought for me in Paris when we knew a certain baby was on the way, were under the table. I picked them up and started to cry.

I looked at the shoes again and dropped face down on the bed. "Mommy, mommy, come to dinner, mommy. Where is daddy? Why isn't daddy coming to supper with us?" "Because daddy is working far away," "Does he send me money?" "Money, you don't know what money is, Bobby." "Yes, I do. Man gives me pennies every day. Look." I reached into his trousers and pulled out a brown coin. "Daddy doesn't send me money, that's why my clothes are torn."

"Bobby, eat your supper, your clothes are torn because you play too hard. Bobby, please don't talk. You talk too much for a little boy, and stop banging your fork." Bobby closed his mouth tightly. He scarcely touched the food on his plate. For the remainder of the meal, he refused to eat. She had heard Marie whispering, "Keep still," as she put down his vegetables. She feared the sort of things. Serving girls who encouraged disrespect under the pretense of cooperation with the parents. She was trying to figure out her budget and the price of Sunnyside nursery school, with a woman to come and evenings when the telephone rang.

The following day was terrifically hard at the office, and I came home to find a telegram from my former husband on the very morning of his arrival that evening. He would just pop up! He wrote, "I want to see my boy the minute I get there." Now suddenly, I traveled all over and had to sit on the edge of the telephone table to keep my knees from giving Morse code. I must be hungry. I meant to have a good lunch as I must be careful not to give way to fainting spells. I walked as fast as I could to the bedroom and began to arrange my hair.

"I won't be nice, and I won't cry; it will be hard on Bobby, but I must not be nice." I looked at the telegram again. He would arrive at the airport, not far from the house, almost immediately. "Bobby Bobby," my voice caught and stopped. Presently, a little voice answered her, and Bobby wandered into her room with Mickey upside down in one arm, "Daddy's coming, Bobby." He looked at her incredulously. "Daddy, your daddy is coming very soon now. Do you want to help me set the table so that Marie can make the supper very nice?" "Bobby, let's go outdoors in the sand pile, and then if daddy is still here tomorrow, you can take him to the sand pile tomorrow you can… "

The doorbell rang, and Bobby ran to the top of the stairs. I felt weak again and sat down in the big chair. There were streaks of joy before Johnny had reached the third landing. That must've been a very long hike, and Bobby saying, and then Johnny saying, "Where's mommy, little man, is she all right?" Johnny came into the room with Bobby, and I felt worse than ever. His face, red from the wind, was the face of someone else. They kissed, and Bobby kept on talking about the sand pile. He was so sweet, he seemed so happy. I shrank back into the chair. "Let's, let's not talk about Bobby," said Bobby, "I don't have to be good, mommy. Daddy is here." I felt an angry surge. Bobby pushed the silver to one side and hit the floor with a bang "Bobby, stop that, if you don't behave yourself, you have to go to your room." "No, I won't," he said, "Daddy is here."

In my dreams, Johnny turned to me and said, "No, you must obey your mother." But he didn't. He didn't do anything. In my fantasy, he then said, "I'm making lots of money and I want to give you 100 a week, will that do?" "I'm making a good salary now," but you must have some things that you want, he must have some clothes, he must travel." Oh no, I shall go on working, oh no, I shall go on working. I didn't know it could be so heavenly to work. My husband became silent; you would have to forget how things were when I left. I couldn't forget that he smiled and put his arm around my neck. But then I came back to the real world, and Johnny said, "Can I borrow a few dollars?" I said "No!" And

I said, "I have a work event tonight. Can you watch Bobby?" And he said, "No!" and left and slammed the door. I tried not to cry.

Suddenly, the phone rang. I did not imagine that the office would call so soon. They all worked hard in that little office together. David, my boss, had asked me to go to a work evening event. We always worked well together and enjoyed working together.

The gentle old lady arrived who would watch Bobby. I touched Bobby's soft little face as tears were running down because his daddy left so quickly. I couldn't console him and

I had to go. I gave him a long, tight hug and ran out.

My boss showed up in a taxi, actually a limousine that floated over the bridge, in a way to make a girl feel ecstatic. "I wouldn't have believed there was a machine like this outside of the Ford Museum," I said. "Hush, the driver will hear," David replied, "Just leave your hand in mine, it's much better that way." I was not sure whether I should be outraged, flattered, scared, or laugh. He was my boss. Finally, I said, "Where are we going? I hope it won't take forever." I had taken a bath and quickly slipped into the only evening dress I possessed, but when I arrived, he was mesmerized by how beautiful I looked. I just responded, "It's from

Paris." He responded with, "We could change taxis," dubiously, "and I could whisk you away to Paris."

He continued, "I can't lose you, my dear, if I have to spank the young boy myself."

"I must see Paris in a new light with you someday. Don't pull away, I'm not kissing your hand, I'm not even saying. We can give the boy to a nurse on the boat. I don't know whether your son would like me," His eyes twinkled, "and I only know that you were pretty sure of yourself and we both needed to dine and dance tonight."

She saw David in the office the next day, and they worked all day and into the late night. When she arrived the next morning, David said we might talk a little later. "I'm very tired this morning, my husband came back last night, and I lied and said, "He wanted me to be his wife again." David's face went white. "Don't talk to me now, don't talk to me here, please." They began to work and worked very hard; there were sales on everything. I found myself checking prices so carefully that the figures became more jumbled. "I can't tell you what to do, it's not like I can play ball with him, or anything, because he doesn't like it, and you think he's too young to be put in school. I just want you to go to the sun garden and take some tea with toast." David said, "Then go along home and wait until I get there. It might be midnight, but I'll come.

There was such a jumble of traffic below that the street seemed even worse than usual. It was very warm. I took my hat and coat off and sat there aching. Of course, this was something strange and an unfamiliar view of things, as I was rushing about madly. I had to get home. I knew in my heart that my boy must have his mother. David took me places, leaving Bobby behind. David and I spent more time together. Absent little children, she had seen with her own eyes during her week's vacation with David, watching other boys play by the sea.

I was in the most stupid way when I prepared a meal for David one evening at my home. I scarcely knew what I was doing as I pulled things out of the parcels to try to arrange a salad so it wouldn't look too dumpy. I was tired as if I had walked 1000 miles, although I had actually ridden the whole way in a taxi. Everything in the apartment was the way Bobby's little hands liked it. The truck was in the window, and some stuffed dogs were on the pillows like a river. I didn't bother to pick things up; I just kept closing doors until only the dining room was open.

In the tiny table, I had put some tinsel from the box of colored balls from Bobby's Christmas tree. It sparkled so magnificently in candlelight. I put them on a reflector and they reminded me of the first time she danced with David. He said that the tall red candles heightened her brilliance, spinning around the room and waving her hands to the music.

When David came to the apartment, he looked tired. His eyes were red, and I thought he was miserable, but he laughed when he saw the table, and he held me very close and asked me not to talk. "I will tell you one thing about the candles on your table, my dearest, one stands for virtue, the other for merciful love." Several mornings later, I sat at the kitchen table with my little boy. It was late, but I would have to continue being late for a while until I explained everything to Bobby. I would after he ate his meal. She was sitting there trying not to appear hurried, telling him patiently that daddy was still his daddy. But now, they would move, and uncle David was going to live with them soon because I was going to marry uncle David. I told him that Bobby would go to a very nice boarding school and make new friends. When he came home for the holidays, there would be a house in the country with servants who were trained.

Then, the reality hit me that if I went with David, if he actually did marry me, I would be in the same place as before. I would not write. Instead, I would be a servant to but another man. I would not ride horses or take walks in the country. My creativity and independence would die. What was I thinking? Was I just marrying him because he was nice? Johnny was nice and loving at the beginning. Johnny promised me everything. David had more money, but was I just a glorified prostitute, paid to be a man's slave? Would he be happy to let me write articles, go to meetings with publishers? Would I be happy? Certainly, Bobby would not. What was I doing? Had I learned nothing?

Right then and there I decided that I had to change my life. I had to be in control, take charge of who I was, where I was, and spend time with my son. Suddenly, I decided that I had to get out of the city, go to the countryside and find a place to relax, think, recuperate, and write.

My sister had been going to the Berkshires in Western, MA, for a couple of summers and asked me to join her there for a visit. She focused on Monterey and Otis, Massachusetts. These were the towns where everyone knew each other, were helpful if needed, but respected your space and privacy. I wanted a place for me to write and a new type of home for Bobby,

I began to write to Johnny about life in a small rural town. Although the letters from Johnny were less frequent, I wrote him almost every day. I wrote to Johnny about how the teachers watch out for the children and their health in these small-town schools.

And many small-town children had a much better education than the inner city. Bobby already had friends in Otis. There were small classes, and the teachers all knew them well. There weren't the city distractions, but good, healthy athletic things to do. In the country, we didn't have to worry about new clothes. I could have a place in Otis for much less money and rent out my place in the city for more than I spend. And you really had no say in the matter anyway. I needed to go there. It was my retreat.

In September, I decided to go off to Otis. Johnny objected strongly to my moving Bobby there for school. But he was in Chicago then, working for the Chicago Sun. He thought it was utterly mad, the idea that it would not be restful, and that Bobby liked it and wanted to ski. He called it gallivanting off to some god forsaken place. And you would all soon miss the city. He really didn't understand Otis. And then he could not understand how he could send something to East Otis, just marked "Otis Stage," and it would get there. He really did not know Otis. How would they find you? "Does the stagecoach delivery know everyone in East Otis?"

"Well, yes!" I replied.

The house in Otis, Massachusetts, was in this small quintessentially New England rural town in the Western hills of

Massachusetts. But there was something unique about the town that attracted people from Boston and New York City. People like me, and people who wanted the woods and the lakes, the solitude, find the privacy not found in other places. The town attracted writers, artists, dancers, art collectors, and journalists who, most of the time, put aside their elitism to blend in with those whose ancestors built the town. In jeans and flannel, snowshoes and boots, canoes and fishing gear, it was sometimes hard to know who you were speaking to, except when a NYC or Boston accent leaked out. Many of those out-of-towners had lived part-time or full-time for forty or fifty years, but they would always be outsiders, like me.

My sister then told me about a nice older man, whose wife had left him and who needed someone to cook for him and clean up. Just to help him out, and in turn, we would have the house to stay in. It was a very clear contractual arrangement with no other expectations. Wilbur Phelps loved the idea of having someone to keep him company and a young boy being in the house, because he never had children and had always wanted them. I worked for Wilbur Phelps, well, if you could call it that. We both wanted company. My assistance would be in lieu of any rent. Wilbur Phelps had 25 acres of land in Otis, MA, on what was now Route 23. The house itself was on a 1-acre lot with a barn, but it was surrounded by 100 acres. There were beautiful trails on his accompanying property and a lake that was pristine and devoid of houses or people. The property had been in his family for generations. It was a great place to think and to write. Johnny was working in Washington, DC at that moment, so there was no need to spend the hot summers in NY.

Otis was a place of cool summer breezes and bright sunshine. A fireplace warmed us at night in the winter. The house needed work, but inside, Wilbur was so excited when I painted it, rearranged the furniture, and added some art to the walls. I loved to cook all kinds of imaginative meals, some of which made it into stories and magazine articles with recipes. It was my sanctuary, and Wilbur and I spent long afternoons and evenings taking walks or telling stories by the fireplace. He was a good bit older than I and reminded me of my Uncle Fitz or my dad. I was from Kansas, so I could help with the chickens and pigs that were on the property, and tend to the garden where I grew lots of herbs and vegetables for cooking. We enjoyed working on our little farm. Wilbur preferred to think of me as a younger sister. Rumors started that we were romantically involved when he deeded the house and one acre of land to me. I told him not to, but he said that he had no other family than me and Bobby. He wanted us to have it and be damned with the rumors. He was the adult support and friendship that I needed, and when Wilbur got ill, I was there for him. I would find herbs for him and talk to nutritionists about what he should eat to be healthy. I had a bicycle and would ride the three miles into town to Bond's to get meats and vegetables or canned goods. He was there for me when I was upset or stressed about Johnny or not getting published. He would take Bobby fishing and spend time with him so that I could have some quiet time to write. It was the closest thing to a dad or grandfather, or uncle that Bobby had ever had. The people in Otis were so different than NYC or Kansas, everyone knew me and offered to help if I needed it. But no one bothered you unless you reached out to them. They always respected your privacy. It was my very special place and always would be. I kept telling Wilbur not to worry about Bobby and me and to just take care of himself, but he would not hear of it. He said that he had no one else and that we were his family. I really did love that man in a very special way. We looked forward to spending time all summer, fall, foliage, or even winter. It looked beautiful during those times of year when there were fewer people around. We would make trails through the woods in the snow, and Wilbur could tell us what kind of animals had left footprints in the snow.

As Wilbur's health worsened, I convinced him to sell off the land and at least spend winters in a community that was more populated. He outright rejected Florida, although he considered traveling cross country with Bobby and me to California when I entertained that thought. He sometimes came and spent a few weeks at my apartment in NYC, which I kept for when I had to go to NYC to meet a publisher. He spent some time in Westchester with a friend, but he would not sell the house and one acre that he had deeded to me. He insisted that it was for me. As the economy had collapsed, and the drought wreaked havoc on the Plains out West, Otis, MA seemed like a place to get away from it all. I could still turn on the radio and pick up a newspaper to find out what was going on in the rest of the world.

I could write articles from the little town.

I could finally find peace and write. No more drama, no more arguing.

I would have a bicycle and ride into town to get my groceries. I could maybe ride horses again, but I felt the freedom I felt back in South Dakota. Maybe I would teach a little, write a little, bring up Bobby.

Sit by the pond on the pier, dangling my feet in the water.

At least in Otis, I could sit by a stream and write poems for the local paper. Words on a page were so much more. They were like the stream itself. They flowed and shifted and changed, bubbled up and crashed over rocks til they all came together to tell our story. I gathered my poems and wrote new ones, letting the pond, the trees, the moon tell the stories of our lives.

FRAIL MOON

Frail moon, paint moon

Gold thin sliced, hung high above

Black trees

Grace Hill, Remote in brooding

you hang light-meshed in veils above

this ridge

 shine soft, O delicate drifter in the sky.

Dear thought, faint thought

My two hands grasp your star tipped shape

slim curve

I hold you close against my heart

and dream…

Above the old walled town

you mount the heavens, you climb

The Liberation of Sue Moody

Til lost in pale green sky

and feathery spray.

Then as you glance once more my way

seeing brown sand along a shore

 you find one dark piece of sorrowing life below

and know -- it's me.

Or this

DUSK

Bring me the shadows

when you come

they would be comfort

when you're gone.

Bring me the moons

slim stem of gold,

it will curve round me when I am old.

Leave spoon of silver

on the hearth

 to speak forever

of your worth

give me an old jug

and a brush

to paint the sunset at days hush

then bring a snatch of soul ,

your smile

and I shall go inside…

a while

then bring a snatch of soul ,

your smile

and I shall go inside…

Chapter 12
The Little House in Otis

The house that Sue Moody lived in was built in 1900 by the Phelps family, when there was only 452 people living in Otis Massachusetts. Being near the road meant that it was easier to get wood to heat the house and get hay for the horses. But this house had no heat, no horses, no electricity. It was a white house by the main road. There was a seat built into the window where she sat and stared at the woods, and dreamed that she could see the lake a mile away. She would sit there writing her poems and stories whose notes were left behind on crumbled paper, in little journals, or story ideas scribbled on the back of an envelope. The windows had munnions that soared high. The upstairs floor had bedrooms that were once alive with voices. A piano used to sit there. She always said that she never played very well, but by playing, she could hear the music of the masters, the orchestra from Tanglewood or Paris, or Italy. The walls of the house were covered with art bought in different corners of Europe from her many trips. One was from her first trip to Paris with Johnny. She had no money at the time, but thought that if she could bring these prints and drawings to New York, someone would want to buy them. She never really sold many, although she needed the money. The house needed major repairs that she could not afford, but she promised herself that one day, she would put all the pieces back together. She came to Otis like so many other out-of-towners and fell in love with the little New England town at a moment when everything in her life was falling apart. In Otis, she could find peace outside and inside. Sue Moody lived in Otis until she was 94 years old.

Sue Moody would come to teach as adjunct faculty at various schools and Universities. She continued to write, especially poetry. Her son Bobby started but never finished his PhD. He was a Communications officer in the Korean War. He settled in Boston, teaching English, and married Delda. They never had children, and he died in 2004, just 8 years after his mother. Delda died 8 years after that. His writings, like those of Sue Moody, were just those left in the piles at the old Wilbur Phelps house. He always referred to himself as growing up in NYC, but the reality was that he went to school and spent much of his formative years in Otis, MA. He went to school at Monument Mountain High School in Great Barrington, MA. He settled in Boston, MA, with his first teaching job and so that he could visit, help his mom, and he always thought that one day they would fix up the house.

They never fixed it up, nor sold the house in Otis. Decades later, the house of Sue Moody is still there, but barely. It stands there as a monument to the serenity of the place, even amid a life crumbling around you. The portico has fallen in on itself, posts are hanging, windows are broken, and the entrance is blocked by debris. The once white house is now a dingy gray remembrance of itself. The attached barn is a shambles of broken wood. All of this is hard to see through the untamed, overgrown bramble and brush. Inside the house, in a corner amongst the mouse droppings, cob webs and fallen timbers, were the piles of boxes which are the source for this book. Along with the thousands of letters and journals were dozens of articles that she had written over the years for newspapers, books, along with recipes, poems, and plays.

Every day, cars stream by the broken house in this little town, barely noticing that it exists. But each day, a new person moves into another house in Otis with their own story, their hopes and dreams. Does it ever matter? Will it ever mean anything? Who will remember? I picture her sitting with her feet dangling by the lake, with her necklace on, looking out at the trees and the rocks and the weeds; the trees and rocks that have witnessed her life. Re-stringing the necklace, which has fallen apart, is much like rebuilding an old house or putting together the gems of a person's life, left in boxes.

Strewn out in front of you, it is hard to conceive of which came first, what was in the middle, and how to hold it all together, in the end, with a clasp. It needs to be put back together if we are to understand Sue Moody's struggle to be a writer, a journalist, and a single mother in the 1930s and 40s. Just as she strung together some cheap beads, she saw its beauty and potential, and she tried to string together a career at a time when a woman was expected to get married and have children. A career as a journalist was out of the question, they told her, but she prevailed, losing everything perhaps, but trying to follow her dreams. She tried to piece it all together, but parents and a husband, society and war disrupted her dreams and fairytale versions of life at every turn. She travelled to Paris many times until she was trapped there while Hitler bombed the city. She wrote food and fashion articles until she had to write about starvation. Unlike a puzzle, there is no set way to put it back together and make sense of it all. There are many outcomes to the order of the necklace and to understanding what happened in her life.

The house is now broken like the necklace, a house begins to fall apart at its seams and the walls start to cave in, and the portico collapses, the roof is ripped and opens light to the sky, and after the paint has peeled away from its very façade, does it still remember who it once was?

Does the house remember her, and is it the culmination of a life once lived? Can we see the beauty of life through the bramble and cobwebs, and fallen timber? Through it all, there is something majestic about remembering a life and what it left for us. Sue Moody left us the letters and journals so that, like the necklace, we can string them back together. She left enough of the pieces of her life that we can reconstruct the life of this woman with beautiful hats, poems, and journals.

Epilogue

It was Memorial Day 1991 in the small town of Otis. The parade consisted of a fire truck, a police car, a couple of antique cars, several veterans marching in uniform, Boy Scouts and 4H Girls. There were about five people on beautifully groomed horses with bows in their mane. Children in brightly colored clothing chased each other or stood holding their mother's hand. I stood there holding onto my 3-year-old son who was mesmerized by the parade, even though it was not even 4 blocks long. We had just moved from New York City, and he had never seen such a parade or such beautiful horses. Suddenly, a very slender elderly woman on a similarly worn bicycle with narrow wheels pulled up alongside us. She had on a beautiful hat with dried flowers on it and wore long white gloves. Her wide blue pants and tucked-in aged white shirt were obviously too big for her slender frame, but she still looked elegant. She stood out from the men in flannel shirts and women in denim and sweats. It was a chilly day in the hills of Otis for a May morning. She came over to us and touched my son's golden blonde ringlet curls. He was obviously in need of a haircut, but I could not bring myself to cut the ringlets that became banana curls. She just said, "What a beautiful little boy." I said thank you, and she walked her bike

The Liberation of Sue Moody

further down the parade route. I always wondered who she was, and I never saw her again.

Years later, I learned that it was Sue Moody. She stayed mostly to herself and few people still remember her, but those who do remember recall that she always wore a stylishly handcrafted hat and rode her bicycle everywhere. She rode the three miles into town every week to, now, Terranova's market, the little general store, to get all of her needs. Folks say that she would sit on her porch and write poetry or tend to the flowers around her. Her poems appeared almost every month in the paper for the town next door, The Monterey News. They can still be found in the library.

Sue Moody left us stories, recipes, articles, and poems.

One of the last poems she wrote was published in the Monterey News:

Great splashes of paints
and fiery red
The autumn goes
like the red rose.
Trying to say good night,
Lost, now with you
  I see the mountains glow

Tawny below

Rose perfume fills my heart

white snow hills stretch

some autumns never go

spite of the crisp snow

I linger on, the words

now escape me

Sunset is giving way

And the red roses have had its day

www.ingramcontent.com/pod-product-compliance
Lightning Source LLC
Chambersburg PA
CBHW040857010826
48978CB00013BA/1060